PRAISE FOR *LEADERSHIP LANGUAGE*

"Chris Westfall helped me develop and deliver the presentation that changed my life."

—**J. Emilio Cano,**
winner on *Shark Tank–Australia,* Season One

"**Great book!** *Leadership Language* is more than a 'how-to' path to superior communication strategies. It's a road map for saving precious time. When everyone is in the same lane, confusion is eliminated, synergy is enhanced, and time is on your side."

—**Vince Poscente,**
New York Times best-selling author of *The Age of Speed*

"**Breakthrough communications strategies** that can change the conversation, and change your results."

—**David Horsager,**
New York Times best-selling author of *The Trust Edge*

"If you want to increase your ability to influence others and make powerful change, read this book now."

—**Dorie Clark,** author of *Reinventing You* and *Stand Out*;
adjunct professor, Duke University Fuqua School of Business

"**Put this one on your list.** Fantastic practical leadership insights and advice from a real pro. Good examples, stories, pacing—high-quality content that is easy to digest. Chris is successful for a reason. In *Leadership Language* he helps you find success, too. Highly recommended."

—**Dr. Todd Dewett,** number 1 most-watched management expert on LinkedIn Learning, TEDx speaker, authenticity expert, and author of *Show Your Ink*

"**Make *Leadership Language* an asset to your organization.** Effective communication is the only way to drive results, operational efficiency, and impact. You have to account for leadership if you want to influence others. This book will show you how to do that, and more."

—**Curt VanderMeer,** president and CEO, Endangered Species Chocolate

"**A remarkable, imaginative, and life-changing book.** During my forty years as a journalist, I simply figured that the great leaders I interviewed all possessed some intangible, unteachable ability to inspire those around them. It just never occurred to me that leadership could be taught. Then I read *Leadership Language*."

—**Skip Hollandsworth,**
executive editor, *Texas Monthly* magazine;
author of *Midnight Assassin* and co-writer of the movie, *Bernie*

"**A brave look at where leadership lives.** This book changes the conversation around impact, and what influence really means. There's never been a greater need for clear-headed leadership, and this book is your access point for new results."

—**Jay Winn,** vice president, Ogilvy New York

"**Masterful.** Chris provides you with simple, powerful, effective strategies for quieting the noise. Read this book and accelerate your leadership transformation."

—**Karen Mangia,**
vice president, Customer and Market Insights, Salesforce

"**Chris has a gift. Period.** What makes Chris unique is his ability in teaching that skill to others."

—**Dr. Brandon Sweeney, PhD,** co-founder of Essentium Technologies and
winner of the Rice Business Plan Competition

LEADERSHIP
LANGUAGE

CHRIS WESTFALL

LEADERSHIP
LANGUAGE

USING AUTHENTIC
COMMUNICATION TO
DRIVE RESULTS

WILEY

Library of Congress Cataloging-in-Publication Data:

Names: Westfall, Chris, author.
Title: Leadership language : using authentic communication to drive results / Chris Westfall.
Description: First Edition. | Hoboken : Wiley, 2018. | Includes index. |
  Identifiers: LCCN 2018021623 (print) | LCCN 2018025120 (ebook) | ISBN 9781119523352 (ePub) | ISBN 9781119523321 (Adobe PDF) | ISBN 9781119523345 (hardback)
Subjects: LCSH: Leadership. | Communication in management. | BISAC: BUSINESS & ECONOMICS / Leadership. | BUSINESS & ECONOMICS / General. | BUSINESS & ECONOMICS / Management.
Classification: LCC HD57.7 (ebook) | LCC HD57.7 .W45587 2018 (print) | DDC 658.4/5--dc23
LC record available at https://lccn.loc.gov/2018021623

Printed in the United States of America

V10003035_080318

For my mom, with love
Gone but not forgotten

CONTENTS

FOREWORD

I have a simple motto hanging in my office:

Success is not about what you work on. It's what you choose NOT to work on.

I've been running different businesses since I was 14 years old. Some have done well, some not so much. If you're anything like me, you're continually looking for a path to success that feels right. A fundamental transformation comes when you finally know you're on the right track. That transformation is what this book is really about.

When I made my first feature film, *Why I'm Not on Facebook*, I planned it out scene-by-scene as though I was on the set of one of my television shows. I spent hours of time (and mountains of money) sweating every shot, scripting every outcome, tweaking every payoff. I had a specific plan, and so that's the movie I set out to make.

When I screened the first cut of the film for my graphics team, my lead editor simply said, *"It's terrible."*

He told me I had created a perfectly structured 90-minute piece of boring crap that nobody would watch. Or believe. He also told me there was only one scene that worked. "The scene with you and your son was the only piece of real filmmaking in the entire project. That's the story you should tell."

I had been telling talent I worked with to "follow the story" and "just be authentic" for so long that I think I forgot what that actually meant. I had just tried to manufacture a story to fit what I wanted people to hear, not what I was authentically trying to say. That never works, and I knew better. It was just harder to see that fact when I was the subject.

So I redid the entire film, with one thing in mind: *authenticity.* I agreed to follow the story wherever it took me and to trust that the audience would understand my journey. I'm thankful every day that my editor was so blunt and honest.

My success with *Bar Rescue, Extreme Makeover, Why I'm Not on Facebook,* and whatever else I've done in this life has come from trusting that true leadership always starts with a leap of faith. Scripting out every angle and every response gets you a plan, but no real impact.

Leadership is as real as it gets. I've learned hard lessons over the years being a CEO and entrepreneur. I've had thousands of employees and made nearly every mistake you can make trying to force leadership on those around me. When I finally learned how to trust my own faults and rely on the people on my team, I allowed myself to be vulnerable and everything changed.

A good leader knows that you can't push, fake, or finesse your way to success. That may sound counterintuitive, coming from someone who works in Hollywood. "Hollywood show business" actually has very little *show* to it. It's a very sensitive and mature marketplace where there is no room for gamesmanship. If the executives and investors smell hype or hyperbole, you're dead in the water.

Authenticity is something you cannot fake and you cannot learn. From employees to customers, people can sense it if you're trying to be something you're not.

Back in the seventies, a common sales strategy was to use the name of the person you were talking to—the prospect—frequently; the thinking was that a person's name was the sweetest sound in the world, so you should use it often.

Now we see that as a HUGE turnoff. It's not special. Not the "sweetest sound." It now effectively has the exact opposite impact than when designed. It's now seen as a technique—a technique for manipulation. And it doesn't work.

Yet there is *science* behind that outdated idea. But when you try to force the outcome by manipulating your audience, the science gets lost. We all want to connect with others in a way that's easy to understand and easy to listen to, but it can never be manipulative.

I know that not every pitch is going to be the next *Bar Rescue* and that every show I make won't save lives like *Extreme Makeover: Weight Loss Edition.* But I go into every project and every challenge in my business with a story that's clear, concise, and real. What about you? How do you bring your story to life?

It's time to change the conversation. It's time to get real; to access a scientific approach to the way things work, so you never have to fake it.

Audiences today are more sophisticated than ever. That's true whether you're talking to a studio exec or to an executive within your company. This book is not about systems and tweaks. It's about taking a candid look at the cards you're holding and deciding how to play them so that you can persuade from a place of *reality*. Not technique.

What I've found is that authenticity, and a willingness to embrace weakness without fear, excuses, or spin, has allowed me to be happier and more emotionally stable. Television can be a fickle mistress, but wherever this journey continues to take me, I'm going there as myself.

And so are you. Chris has created a road map to help you find what's missing, and that journey starts on the inside. It's not about being scripted, it's about embracing the unknown—ignoring what doesn't matter, so you can capture what does.

INTRODUCTION

I've watched lots of leaders—and aspiring leaders—struggle with expressing their vision. The difference between struggle and success is your story. I wrote this book because I believe that you have a story to tell. A story that connects you to the people who matter most, and to the results you need.

But life isn't just a story you write. It's a conversation you live.

Wouldn't it be great if you could say to your team, your competition, or your board of directors, "Shhh now, I have a story to tell!"

That's not how life works.

Life (and leadership) is a dialogue.

If you are reading this book, you are going to get the real story on leadership. You're going to understand how to change the *conversation*—and change your results.

Sir Kenneth Branson said, "Communication is the greatest skill any leader can possess." I believe that, because I have seen it. In my work with tens of thousands of entrepreneurs, executives, and business leaders, I've seen how effective communication—or the lack of it—has driven results, sometimes into the stratosphere ... sometimes into the ditch.

Note that for every mile of road, there are two miles of ditch. So choose your words (and your conversations) carefully.

Communication will create the results you need, or the consequences you don't. If you aspire to inspire, take time to consider carefully how you bring your story to life.

Over the last several years, I have been on a journey of personal and professional discovery. Searching for new avenues of peak performance, I turned to a variety of gurus and guidance as part of an exploration into the leadership mind-set. I wanted to know:

- What makes an effective leader?
- What makes *me* effective (and ineffective) as a leader?
- Are those factors the same for everyone, or is leadership a function of personality, perseverance, charisma, background . . . or something else?
- Can anyone be a leader?
- How can people access whatever leadership skills exist inside and bring those skills to life for the teams they care about?

At first, it looked like there was a hidden "leadership process" that I didn't quite understand, or that I hadn't quite implemented. But something didn't feel right.

In spite of my lack of knowledge, I had managed to build and lead teams around the world as a senior executive in technology and consumer brands. As a consultant, I had led entrepreneurs to find new results, access new funding, and deliver new ideas for dozens of ventures. I had helped my clients to create unprecedented results, transforming their careers and their lives in the process. I provided communications workshops to Fortune 100 companies, introduced insights to rocket scientists at Sandia National Laboratory, and worked with the U.S. Navy SEALs.

Yet that experience didn't seem to matter. Instead of confidence and new discovery, the gurus gave me self-doubt.

The hidden leadership process began with a fundamental premise: I lacked something.

Leadership was like baking a cake: you simply had to understand the recipe and the process. And, according to "expert sources," I didn't have the cookbook, or even the right ingredients. Leadership was something "out there"—something out of reach.

According to the experts, despite my results and my beliefs to the contrary, I was flawed. Something was missing.

Of course, the leadership books and gurus I turned to had the answer, and the recipe, for that missing ingredient. But something in the kitchen didn't smell right.

I knew I wasn't broken. And neither are you.

I didn't need to be flawed in order to want to be more, achieve more, and see greater impact. I had seen Millennials, with minimal experience, lead others to maximize their results. I had been a part of transformations that cut across industry lines, age, gender, and other barriers to bring powerful stories to life.

I discovered that I didn't need a six-step process, or 21 irrefutable laws, to be a leader. I simply needed a greater understanding of the place where leadership lives. I needed to look in the direction of real impact, if that was what I wanted to create for my business, my clients, and my life.

You may be expecting a recipe for leadership: "*Do these things and see these results.*" Let's look at those expectations.

Have you ever followed a guru's advice, and achieved different results? You said their words but obtained your own outcomes?

Why is that? Maybe leadership isn't a recipe. Maybe it's time to concentrate on where real results come from. When you *discover* new things, when you *understand* new things, you will see new results.

This book is a journey of personal discovery, not just tips and techniques, because tips and techniques will only take you so far.

Focusing on tips and techniques is like putting lightning-fast, highly efficient wheels on a stagecoach. No matter how well you engineer those wheels, that stagecoach isn't going to get you on the highway. You can add six horses—or even sixty. Now your solution is well-engineered, efficient, and exceeding typical expectations within the stagecoach community. But you can't even get on the entrance ramp to the freeway. And there's no way you're going to get to Hawai'i or Dublin, unless you're already in those places right now.

Guidance often focuses on improving your wheels. And that's what I did for a long time: I wanted to make stagecoach drivers more efficient. I wanted to help horses run faster and hold those horses accountable for their results. Sound familiar?

Fortunately, there's more to the story.

Let me introduce you to the vehicle that will really get you where you want to go. That's the focus of *Leadership Language*: the intrinsic and powerful source of innovation, inspiration, and impact.

Stop looking at improving the wheels on your stagecoach: you're looking in the wrong direction.

When it comes to leadership, the real secret isn't in the cart or the horse.

If you'll quit fixing your wheels, you will see it.

When I began my career working for Fortune 100 companies, I was trapped in a stagecoach, trying to maximize the performance of my horses. I was trying to create incremental improvements and efficiencies that would add value to my team and to the company's bottom line. I believed the gurus, and I was locked into yesterday's news. I was looking in the wrong direction. I wasn't looking in the direction of leadership. Not for myself. Not for my board. Not for my team.

You deserve more. You deserve a fresh perspective. A perspective that comes from inside of you. In this book you will learn:

- How to tap into your innate leadership skills and bring your vision to life

- How to access an ease and authentic confidence that can change your results

- The language that is the source of real connection, influence, and impact
- A deeper understanding of how authenticity, trust, and vulnerability are your superpowers and the building blocks of new outcomes
- What you can do, right now, to live your authentic story—and lead others to do the same

This book isn't about incremental improvements and making your cart go a little faster. *Leadership Language* asks you to step out of the stagecoach and onto a new stage.

Change the conversation and change your results. This book will show you how.

Leadership is about transformation—and that transformation begins right now.

1 When Leaders Can't Lead

The dry conditions were just right for a forest fire. And that's exactly what broke out in the Helena National Forest, in an area of the world known as Mann Gulch.

Fourteen firefighters were called in to put out what they believed to be a "10 o'clock fire." A 10 o'clock fire, in the parlance of the forestry service, means a fire that will burn itself out by 10 o'clock the next day.

It had been an especially long, hot summer in Montana. On this August day in Missoula, the mercury topped 97 degrees Fahrenheit. It was the hottest day of the year.

The leader of the team was a gentleman named Wagner Dodge. Dodge was the oldest and most experienced of the group. So, naturally, he was in charge. Because of experience. Right?

Most of the men were between the ages of 18 and 28, what we might classify as Millennials, based on their age. Many had seen active military service. These men climbed aboard a C-47 transport plane for the 100-mile flight from Missoula to Mann Gulch. Flying over the flames, the men saw the small fire burning near the river—easily contained. Easily managed.

However, the temperatures were so high on this particular day that the plane had to climb to an altitude of 2,000 feet (instead of the normal 1,800 feet) for the parachute jump. As a result of the higher altitude, or the temperature, or some other unknown reason, one chute did not open. Their communications equipment fell swiftly to the ground, instantly and irreparably crushed on impact.

The men landed in Mann Gulch at 4:10 p.m.

Upon arrival, Wagner Dodge met with his second-in-command, a gentleman named Harrison. Harrison, a ranger stationed in the Helena National Forest, was the first to spot the fire.

Right after their initial meeting, at 4:10 p.m., Dodge and Harrison made their first leadership decision. That decision? Separate themselves from the team. They went off together and had a little dinner. The leaders ate first, a departure from military tradition, while the men waited.

At 5:40 p.m., Dodge and Harrison led the men down into Mann Gulch, an area of the world that's characterized by hidden ravines inside a valley near the Missouri River.

At 5:40 p.m., Wagner Dodge saw something he didn't expect. Flames!

Not six feet high.

Not sixteen feet high.

But sixty feet high.

The men were on a ridge, heading into the gulch, when the wind shifted. A strong downdraft blew the fires up the 18 percent grade, toward the men. Snaking through the dry trees, the once-hidden flames revealed themselves in an instant. The path to the river was blocked.

In mere moments, Dodge and his team were surrounded (on three sides) by flames, advancing at a rate of 200 feet per minute. The only escape? Run uphill, away from the river, to the top of the ridge. On an 18 percent grade. In two-and-a-half-foot-tall grass.

The firefighters were trapped.

Two men found themselves standing near a crevasse. Abandoning their group, they shimmied through a narrow opening to safety—and survival.

Dodge headed for the high ground, yelling at his 13 remaining men to follow him. Dodge knew that he had to do something. Wagner Dodge cried out to anyone who could listen: "Men! Men! Drop your tools!"

Could the men even hear their leader's voice over the sound of the flames? The wind? The exploding trees? The men did not listen ... they could not listen. The fear. The fire. The utter shock at their circumstances.

Running uphill from the flames, Dodge suddenly stopped. He reached into his pocket. At that moment, Wagner Dodge pulled out a pack of matches.

Matches? In the middle of a forest fire?

Wagner Dodge struck a match. Reaching down, he began lighting fire to the tall grass all around him. He moved in a circle, burning the grass quickly to ashes.

Wagner Dodge somehow knew that you could fight fire with fire. And burning the grass all around him was his only path to safety.

He continued to cry out to his men, begging them to join him. Join him in the middle of his own private forest fire.

None of them did.

And as the flames grew closer and closer to Wagner Dodge, suddenly there was nothing left to burn. The flames stopped at the edge of the burnt grass.

Dodge laid down in the middle of his ashen circle. Alone. In the middle of the burnt grass, safe from the flames, Wagner Dodge survived the Mann Gulch Fire. Thirteen of his men, including Ranger Harrison, did not.

We know from the hour and the minute hand on Harrison's broken wristwatch what time the men expired.

5:56 p.m.

From 5:40 to 5:56 p.m.: sixteen minutes. Sixteen minutes of pandemonium. Sixteen minutes of terror.

Sixteen minutes where nothing made any sense.

Ultimately, it took 450 men five days to put out this "10 o'clock fire." On this fateful day, August 5, 1949, a leader had the right idea, at the right time. Yet, the cautionary tale of the Mann Gulch Fire is the quintessential story of a failure in leadership. A failure to connect. A failure to communicate when the stakes were highest.

What happened? And what can we learn from this story of a leader with the right idea, but the wrong result?

In his retrospective, "The Collapse of Sensemaking in Organizations," Karl Weick points out the confusion for the men. Weick points to the elements that led to the men's demise: an uncertainty about their leadership. What kind of leader would ask firefighters to drop their tools—removing their only defense against the blaze? How serious can this fire really be if our leaders go eat supper while the flames are burning? The focus of the team is on unity—yet, the three men who survived did so because they abandoned the team (the two men who escaped through a crevasse) or the team abandoned them (Wagner Dodge).

Ultimately, the men's understanding of the way things worked was challenged. They confronted the unexpected, and they failed.

In other words: the wind shifted, and nothing looked the same. No one was equipped to deal with the change. Except the leader. Alone with his idea—the right idea.

The results on that ridge were not the leader's fault. But they were his responsibility.

What will you do, and what will you say, when the wind shifts? *Leadership Language* will equip you with the skills to deliver your message—to create influence in the face of uncertainty. You will see how to change the conversation and change your results.

As you consider the story of the Mann Gulch Fire, what comes up for you when you consider the idea of trust? Connection? Crisis? And what comes to mind for your team members?

The crazy thing is how this story from 70 years ago, from a remote location in Montana, is really the story of all of us. We are all only moments away from some unexpected shift. A competitor's move. An employee's departure. A surprising technological advance. We live in an era of rapid and constant change, and we work hard to minimize the surprises. But what shows up, in spite of our efforts?

Life. Life shows up. And it's up to you, as a leader, to show up ready to help others to understand how things work.

Guidance in the midst of unexpected change is the need, and the new normal. The words you choose and the actions you take will teach people how to follow your ideas. How to connect with your vision. How to engage with your innovation. Or not.

Today, leaders must have more than the right idea. Ideas without action are just dreams. Ideas without action are what happened in Montana. The good news is: Shifting winds don't have to create disaster. You can have the right idea at the right time and get the right result.

That's why this book is here: to help you to understand how to create results when the stakes are highest. Results for your team. Your organization. Your clients. Your employees. To understand more about the way to make your message matter.

Because no matter what your circumstances or where you are in your life, leadership starts with your story. Leadership is not a title nor a status. Leadership is seen in *action*. It sounds counterintuitive, and it's not what they teach you in English class, but here it is just the same: Leadership is a verb.

Leadership is demonstrated in action, in *connection*, every day. Those connections bring your story to life, for yourself and for those around you. In my work with thousands of business leaders, from Fortune 100 companies to start-up entrepreneurs, I've shared how to turn insights into action. My intention is to share what I see and what I have researched, to help you to see things differently. For yourself. For your career. For the people who matter most to you.

Resources

McLean, Robert. *Young Men and Fire*. Chicago: University of Chicago Press, 1992.

Rothermel, Richard C. *Mann Gulch Fire: A Race That Couldn't Be Won*. Washington, DC: U.S. Department of Agriculture, May 1993.

Weick, Karl E. "The Collapse of Sensemaking in Organizations: The Mann Gulch Disaster," *Administrative Science Quarterly*, Volume 28, 1993.

2 Where Leadership Lives

"A person can have the greatest idea in the world. But if that person can't convince enough other people, it doesn't matter."

—Gregory Berns, neuroscientist

She wanted to win. She didn't know how, exactly. But if she was going to play the game, she was going to play for keeps.

When I met McCalley Cunningham, she was just a college freshman. A freshman with an idea. She wanted to pitch her idea to investors, to see what kind of interest she could gain for her business. She enrolled in a program designed to help entrepreneurs bring their ideas to life.

And that's where we met.

A pitch competition, open to all 65,000 students at her university—one of the largest in the country—would help her to know whether she had what it took. She wanted to take away the prize money. And I had the good fortune of serving as her coach in the process.

She didn't come from anyplace special. She grew up on a farm outside a small town in Central Texas called Iola. When you asked her a question, she answered with a sincere and crisp, "Yes, sir."

She had been successful in Future Farmers of America (FFA). Her email handle introduced her as "goat girl." She was bright. She had storytelling skills that she wanted to develop, because she knew that victory was going to take more than just a great story. In order to be the best of the best, it was going to take more than a well-rehearsed pitch.

McCalley's company had developed a technology that was helping fruits and vegetables to stay fresher, longer. The impact for restaurants, consumers, and the multi-billion-dollar grocery industry was staggering. What if you could increase the shelf life of produce in a grocery store? What would that mean to inventory turns, shipping times, and the razor-thin margins in the grocery business? What if you could safely keep fruits from rotting, just by using a simple and proven science?

I was intrigued.

As a coach to entrepreneurs at the fifth-largest university in the United States, I've had the opportunity to work with thousands of innovative leaders. From student start-ups to *Shark Tank*, my strategies have helped raise over $50 million in business investment as I write these words. I've helped restructure brands on four continents, and each year I work with thousands of senior executives and C-suite leaders. And now, at last, I had the opportunity to work with the Goat Girl.

What could she possibly know about entrepreneurship, technology, and innovation? That's what she wanted to find out.

We quickly saw that innovation doesn't come from what you already know. So her background and experience were neither an asset nor a liability. They were simply part of the past. McCalley wanted to create the future. Can you relate to that impulse?

I appreciated her diligence and her willingness to learn. Most of all, she put ideas into action. As the competition drew nearer, her ideas began to come to life.

The day of the competition finally arrived, and the camera crew began setting up in the George H.W. Bush Presidential Library and Museum, inside the Annenberg Theater. Filmed in front of a live studio audience, filled with approximately 500 community leaders, distinguished alumni, and students, a team of celebrity investors would evaluate the pitches—looking for the best of the best.

At this event, I not only coached all the participants, but I was also the host of the show. When it was time to take the stage, no one expected what happened next.

Poised and professional, McCalley shared her story.

We had worked extensively on Q&A, devising conversational strategies that would bring her ideas to life, even in the face of resistance, tough questions, and potential misunderstanding. She had to lead a group of investors to a new perspective on her business idea.

Her pitch went flawlessly: the eye contact, the engagement with the judges, the key business drivers. It was time for Q&A—the part of the presentation (and of your life) that you can't really rehearse.

Instead of stress, there was ease. The conversation flowed naturally, even when the questions weren't easy. She shared her vision with clarity, making her points quickly and responding to the feedback she received. McCalley was speaking the language of leadership.

No one knew her age. No one knew that she was just a freshman.

No one cared. The judges and the audience were asking more important questions: *How can you help us? How can you help the marketplace?*

She had an innovative solution, and the ability to prove it. Was that going to be enough? Turns out, it was.

It was a great thrill to announce McCalley as the winner of the pitch competition. The MBAs and PhDs who competed that day were disappointed, but not surprised.

Looking back, I reflected on what she had accomplished:

- She was the youngest person ever to take first prize.
- She had beaten graduate students, PhD candidates, engineers, and MBAs.
- She didn't let her age, her experience, or anything else take her away from what she set out to do.
- She had to prove that a technology was compelling, even though it was unfamiliar to the judges and scientists in the room.
- She overcame difficult questions ("Why hasn't someone else thought of this before?" was just one of them).
- She didn't let her inexperience keep the judges from experiencing what they needed to know in order to make a decision. Can you relate?

What was it, exactly, that led to victory?

- Her determination?
- Her focus?

Well, yes. And no.

Of course McCalley was determined and focused. So was everyone else.

Her success, as a leader, came from beyond the words she chose. The place she spoke from was a place of authentic passion, dedication, perseverance . . . the place where *Leadership Language* really lives.

McCalley looked beyond her experience. She looked beyond her words. From a place of connection, and intention, she delivered her message. That place—that place of creation and impact—is the source of real influence and real change. From an internal connection, language overcomes the impossible, brings your experience to life, and brings you (and your team) in touch with your potential.

But if you're looking for magic words, you're going to be disappointed.

You won't find goofy acronyms, guru commandments, or magic words that will cause "leadership" to suddenly appear.

Here's why: you don't need any of that stuff.

Leadership is already here. You just need to know where to look.

Think about children playing on the playground. Do they stop and consider: "Do I really have what it takes to lead?"

Of course not! They start playing tag, or hide-and-seek, or whatever game makes sense at that moment. I remember sitting in a park in downtown Philadelphia and watching a group of kids craft an elaborate game that involved crowns, magic wishes, and some other stuff I couldn't quite understand. But they did, and they had a blast just making things up. Sometimes, one girl would be the queen. And then the other girl would be the queen. Or maybe she was Elsa from *Frozen*? I wasn't quite sure. But I digress. . . .

In business, we have a sense of obligation. Of professionalism. Of propriety. These sentiments often lead us to stop having fun and stop being ourselves.

Why?

Why did you stop being the leader?

Because third grade? Because recess ended? Because you need to be a grown up? Because someone else decided she was the queen?

Maybe it's time to look in a new direction.

Look, I'm not suggesting that we should take recess, play tag, and then push each other into the bushes as a leadership strategy. But there's something beyond all the grown-up obligations that points to what we often forget. Maybe we should look at where we started, to see how the journey can really unfold.

No matter your role, your age, or your title:

We are all of us, in our own way, leaders.

Take the leadership quiz. Ask yourself *whether* you believe the following:

- You want to persuade and influence others.
- You want that influence to be authentic and real, not pushy or manipulative.
- You want your ideas to be heard.
- You want to make an impact.
- You understand that life is about service: What you can do for others is how you create value in your life.

Here's what I believe to be true:

- You have ideas.
- Ideas that need to be heard.
- If your ideas aren't heard, and understood, you're not contributing at your highest level.

That's called your potential.

Funny thing about your potential: Do you know where it is? Where does your potential live, exactly?

It's not "out there." Copying the habits of highly effective people isn't the same as developing your own habits based on your intuition and insight. If you want something or someone to copy, I'm not sure that this is the right book for you. Models are useful, but leadership isn't about imitation.

This book focuses on *your* potential, specifically, your leadership potential. Millennial. Gen X. Baby Boomer. Or even if you are just a big baby. All are welcome.

Your potential depends not only on your ideas, but on your ability to convince others that your ideas are worthwhile.

Meaningful.

Important.

Stella Adler, the acting coach of Marlon Brando, Warren Beatty, and Robert De Niro, among many other performers, famously said that just having great ideas isn't enough. "You've got to have a talent for your talent," was the way she put it. I'd like to add "a talent for serving others."

Leadership is that talent for your talent that helps the people you care about the most. Leadership is about persuasion and influence—sharing your ideas in a way that inspires others to take action. True influence is never "because I said so"—it's because you see what's best for those you wish to inspire. Those you wish to serve.

But leadership is more than inspiration. Leadership is more than making others feel good. The *service* you provide to others is the way your leadership impact will be measured, rewarded, and recognized.

Leadership is about helping others to do the most good.

You're frustrated right now though, because there's a disconnect between who you are and what you know you can contribute. Your potential remains a mystery. Frustration has taken its place.

You owe it to yourself to stop feeling frustrated. If there's something that you want for yourself, and it's not showing up, you have to wonder what you're doing to keep it out.

What does it take to be an effective leader?

Going Beyond Limitations

Do you think you are too inexperienced, too experienced, or too whatever, to create real change?

Well, guess what? Me, too. And McCalley. And everybody else.

We're all too fat, too short, too tall, too disadvantaged in some way or another. Too Millennial. Not a Millennial. Gen Z. Gen X. Whatever.

And yet, in spite of those facts, here we are. I will push on, in spite of my imperfections and differences. How about you?

Do you think that the people eating at Red Lobster realized that their waiter would one day grow up to be Daymond John, the founder of FUBU and a star of *Shark Tank*? Yep, that was one of his first jobs—waiting tables at Red Lobster. The stories of those who have overcome their circumstances are many, and you will read more of them in this book.

But the real story is: What are you doing to overcome your circumstances and help others to do the same?

Leaders are willing to do what others don't, or won't, or can't.

Leaders look at what's missing, and wonder, "What if . . . ?"

"Trust that little voice inside your head that says, 'What if . . .' and then: DO IT."

—DUANE MICHAELS, PHOTOGRAPHER

There are thousands of stories of people who achieved unexpected results and helped others to do the same, in spite of their background, experience, or education.

If you are in charge of a team that's much older than you are—or much younger than you are—or some combination thereof, you owe it to yourself to realize your potential. And to help those around you to do the same.

It's easy to see that age, gender, race, and religion separate us. That's noticing the obvious, not the important. What do you see beyond our differences?

If leadership is about building bridges (and by the way, leadership *is* about building bridges), you have to see beyond generational gaps, gender gaps, orientation gaps, and any other gap that separates you from the people you serve.

Leadership is about connection. Gaps are about separation.

Today we have more ways than ever to connect. But are you making the connections that matter?

The leaders I work with know how to get out of their own way. How to leverage the past, and not be consumed by it. How to do less, to become more.

That place is called your *potential*. And sharing that potential with others is the key to your impact in every facet of your life, your career, and your relationships.

You have resources and skills that you don't even realize. I'm not trying to pump you up or motivate you with a pretty lie. You've probably read that book already, and it didn't work.

I'm simply telling you what I know to be true. I'm telling you what I see inside of every one of the thousands of clients I serve every year: resourcefulness. It's a resource we all share. There's no statute of limitations on good ideas. You can have as many as you like, and never run out.

If that doesn't seem to be true, keep reading. More ideas are on their way.

Anyone who tells you that he or she has the formula for leadership is a liar.

Here's what I will tell you: YOU have the formula for leadership. You just don't know it yet. Nothing to memorize. Only new ideas to discover.

In the middle of a team meeting or heated argument with your CFO, are you telling me that you want to call up some six-step strategy from a book you read? Are you going to go into "Attack Pattern Delta-9" when the going gets tough?

No. Not if you want to succeed. That's not how life works.

As heavyweight boxing champion Mike Tyson said, "Everyone has a plan. Until they get punched in the face."

We take in ideas. Memorizations. Mantras. But knowledge is not the same as insight. Recalling your knowledge of boxing isn't the best way to deal with a punch. You have to face life, in the moment, as it comes.

Leadership comes from the inside out—influenced by training, experience, and learning—but ultimately, you are the only one who can really decide what leadership means. Leadership, like your potential, comes from inside of you.

Underneath your experience, your setbacks, your frustration, and your disappointment, there's something else. Something more. Something that's waiting to come out. When you look inside, you may not see the resourcefulness you possess.

Resourcefulness is a part of the human condition. Just like ten fingers and ten toes, we all have it. Tapping into that resourcefulness and sharing your leadership vision with others is the key to your impact. And my intention. There may be lists, guidance, and advice, but ultimately, it's what you see for yourself that will lead you on your journey.

For example, there's something, right now, that if it were to show up, the game would change. Maybe that game-changer is:

- Hiring a new VP of operations
- Becoming the new VP of operations
- Winning the championship
- Gaining a new client
- Securing a new investment for your idea
- Reaching 10,000 followers on Instagram

Whatever you see that's missing for yourself and the people around you: Let's start there.

Takeaways

- Leadership is a look at your potential. Self-leadership starts the journey, and impact is the destination.

- Leaders are focused on service and helping others to do the most good.

- Leadership is a journey of discovery—not imitation. Innovation doesn't come from what you already know.

- Leaders want to win, and they explore new resources to find new results.

- Resourcefulness is a part of who you are.

- Consider the labels you have for yourself: Are you too young, too old, too inexperienced . . . to have great ideas? To share your ideas with others in a way that creates an impact?

- There's no limit on with who or how you share your gifts, if you're willing to look in that direction.

3 Going Beyond Your Strengths

"It ain't what you don't know that can hurt you. It's what you know for sure, that just ain't so."

—Mark Twain

"**E**rik, why are we speaking English today?"

My coaching client was a super-smart Millennial engineer from Hungary who spoke five languages. Without missing a beat, he said, "Because that's the only language you understand."

Of course. He was speaking *my* language. Because leadership language speaks your *client's* language.

Let me clarify the word "client."

Of course, a client is someone who buys your products and services (that's an external client). You could also substitute the word *customer.* But be careful: The language of leadership is about more than sales. Certainly, sales leaders need to understand how to change the conversation. Sales is an after-effect of leadership—we have to look at the cause if we want to create the effect.

You know you have internal clients: the people on your team, your board of directors, your vendors and suppliers, your boss.

Your client, in the context of this book, means someone whom you serve.

It might be useful to think of your client as your *most important person.* You want to choose your words and actions very carefully when it comes to your most important person. Here's why:

Your client is the source of your success.

Your ability to deliver results, your ability to generate revenue, your ability to advance in your career, your ability to grow your business—it all comes from your clients.

Your personal success—in all aspects of your life, not just in business—hinges on what you create *with, through, and for others.*

Clients are all around you.

Looking beyond your strengths, skills, and talents: What matters most to the people you serve? What's the impact that *they* seek?

Speak your clients' language. It's the only one they really understand.

Creating incremental improvements for yourself and the people around you is called *management.* You manage your career, you manage your team, you manage your organization, and you manage expectations. Management is doing things right. And when you do things a little better, and help others to do the same, you're a good manager.

Leadership, as Peter Drucker famously said, isn't about doing things right. It's about doing the right things. Drucker, author of 39 books including *Concept of the Corporation,* laid the foundation for modern management.

Today, we need to build on his foundation if we're going to discover new insights. That's why I'd like to take Drucker's definition one step further:

Leadership is about doing things right for the clients you serve.

Leadership is the space beyond incremental growth.

Leadership is about insight. And that insight comes from inside. Because you may make mistakes (we all do) and you know that "doing things right" may or may not get you to your results. What looks like a mistake might just be an important course correction. The real mistake might be the label that you're applying to your situation. Let me explain.

I thought I had made a huge mistake when I took on a full-time position with a company in Houston. The CEO told me he needed me in a full-time role, running his sales operations, reporting directly to the president. I told him that was a bad idea.

I was working as a consultant, speaking and writing. I didn't need a job. I had been hired as a consultant to take a look at his sales team and their leadership, and the assignment was going just fine.

Seemed like his suggestion was a mistake, and I told him so. "No, I'm not interested," I said.

He said, "What would it take?" Hmmm. I didn't see that one coming.

On the back of a napkin, I wrote down a number; it wasn't a ridiculous number, but it was an attractive one.

To my surprise, the CEO said, "Done. When can you start?"

You're probably wondering where the mistake comes into play.

Fewer than 100 days later, the CEO called me into his office. I had moved my family to Houston just six weeks before. "I'm afraid it's just not working out," he said. "I'm going to have to let you go."

I felt the blood rush to my face—a reminder of what a huge mistake I had made! This was a mistake with a capital "M"! How did I—how did we—not see it sooner?

Of course it's not working out, I thought to myself. I had told him that it wasn't a good idea, I wasn't a fit for the role or the industry, and yet we moved forward. Some people just don't listen to their consultants.

I saw clearly that the money wasn't my only bottom line. Have you been there? More importantly, I had just moved my family. I'm no stranger to deals that don't work out—that happens all the time—but now: What was the deal for my wife . . . and my kids?

I had a difficult conversation ahead: I had to tell my wife that moving our family was a huge *mistake*. Taking this executive position was a *mistake*. How was I going to fix this? My career had suffered a minor earthquake. I knew I would survive. But was I about to deliver a message that would destroy my marriage?

Here's how this "mistake" played out:

The CEO was a mensch, and he made sure I was taken care of financially. I respect him to this day for the way he handled things. He made sure he fulfilled our financial agreement, and then some.

But having money in your wallet isn't the same as having a happy home life.

I drove around town for two hours, trying to find the words (and the courage) to talk to my wife. What would she say?

There are few conversations that make me nervous, but this one did. My voice was quivering. My hands were shaking. My mistake was a heavy burden. Finally, after burning a few gallons of gas on Houston's highways, I found the courage to enter my driveway in the middle of the day.

I laid out my mistake and watched for my wife's reaction.

"Well," she said as she took a deep breath, " just don't ask me to move."

Wait—What? That was it?

Where were the threats, the scolding, the punishments? Where was the "You made a huge mistake!" monologue that I knew was coming?

Nowhere to be found.

The "mistake" turned out to be financially and personally beneficial to me and my family. We had found a new home in a new city, and those discoveries were not mistakes.

The company was fair, we said our goodbyes on good terms, and I returned instantly to my work as a speaker and consultant. It was a ninety-day detour and an exploration—not a mistake!

If you're going to go beyond your strengths, you've got to take a look at the labels that you're creating, and "mistake" is the first one that needs to go away. Am I suggesting that you are perfect? That you are a leader who is incapable of making a mistake?

Why don't you take the lead on that one and decide for yourself? Was your marriage a "mistake"? Was buying that business a "mistake"? How many regrets would you like to create for yourself?

Labeling something as a "mistake" makes you miss the message within your circumstances. That message might just be that your "mistake" is a gift—a course correction you needed. But if you don't see that need, you call a change a "mistake."

Would you be willing to go through an exercise to replace out-dated labels with a new kind of understanding? It's time to leave the mistakes behind and start looking at your strengths. But first: if you hate books that ask you to write things down, then don't. Don't open up a window in Google docs if that would cause you pain, and don't speak any new ideas into your phone.

However, if you're open to it, this exercise might be useful to record in some way. Are you ready to take the ride?

In order to make it completely painless, let's begin with a simple question:

What are your greatest strengths?

You probably already know what makes you an effective leader. Maybe you've even taken the *StrengthsFinder 2.0* assessment, or you've used other tools, to identify these key characteristics.

Make three columns in a document. Put your strengths in the left column, like this:

1. My Greatest Strengths		

Write down three to five of your greatest strengths. These are your individual strengths. If you're doing this activity with a group, you may want to focus on the strengths of your organization.

Choose the words that will help you most. Ask yourself and your team: Why do you win?

See whether you can come up with one or two that are "off the grid"—in other words, something beyond the assessments. Write down some characteristics that you've heard from others or that you believe to be true about yourself. If you are an "Achiever" or "Developer" in the Clifton Strengths Assessment, what other qualities do you see as your personal strengths? If your company is known for innovation or expertise, what else shows up for you?

Here are some quick ways to identify your strengths:

- What do people tell you that they appreciate about you?
- What qualities contribute most to your success?
- What makes you an effective leader?

Once you're satisfied with your list, create the next column, your *Method of Delivery*. In other words, how do you *transfer* your strengths?

1. My Greatest Strengths	2. My Method of Delivery (Transfer)	
Integrity		
Experience		
Follow-through		
Creativity		
Quality		

For this column, you have to think like someone from the state of Missouri—the Show Me State. It's not enough to say that perseverance is strength, you have to *demonstrate* it. Typically, folks in operations focus on this column, because delivery is how business gets done. How do you deliver your strengths? In a conversation? At a trade show? Via your drivers, dockworkers, and customer service personnel?

Words like compassion, integrity, empathy—these are valuable leadership characteristics and important strengths. But our job is not to simply identify the intangibles of leadership. Concepts are great, if we are making a poster with an image of an eagle on it. ("INTEG-RITY"—can you see what I'm saying?)

Look beyond the concept to consider something more valuable:

Leadership language is not conceptual. It's actual.

That might be an actual eagle in front of an actual mountain, with the actual word "INTEGRITY" written in bold letters. But a picture of a concept isn't the same as the actual thing itself. The map is not the territory.

Inspiring posters are called "decoration," not leadership. Decoration is not delivery. Even for a florist, a designer, or a decorator!

"Our greatest obligation is not to confuse slogans with solutions."
                              —Edward R. Murrow, broadcast journalist

Your strengths have to be demonstrated in action. Otherwise, your strengths are just a test result, or a creative writing assignment. On a poster. With an eagle.

Concepts are important, but if this book only offers concepts, how will you or I deliver meaningful change?

Leadership is about taking action and delivering on your strengths.

Consider your operations. Your interactions. The people on your team. How do you transfer your skills in tangible ways?

Sometimes people deliver their strengths through their employees. Perhaps you use actual delivery trucks, logistics, shipping containers, or other methods of sending your products to your clients. Perhaps you deliver through telephone conversations or a call center. Perhaps your services take place online, in a hair salon, or in a retail store or via blueprints, contracts, and other documents.

Remember, transfer involves doing something: connecting, communicating, engaging, and interacting, as part of your operations.

Now consider the third and final column.

1. My Greatest Strengths	2. Method of Delivery	3. How Is Your Client Better Off?
Integrity	Client Meetings	
Experience	Blueprints/Drawings	
Follow-through	Client Service	
Creativity	R&D/Engineering	
Quality	Installers/Face2Face	

For this one, you need to adopt the perspective of your *client*. Put your ego on hold for a second and think like a client. Shift your perspective; adopt theirs instead.

Now, reviewing your strengths, and your method of delivery: *How is your client better off?*

If you say, "We make more money!" in column three, that's not an outcome for *the client.* That's an outcome for you, and your business. Try again.

Maybe the word "because" can help. When you say, "Because of our strengths and our method of delivery, our *client makes more money,*" now you are on the right track.

You have your strengths. You have your method of delivery. What does your *client* have? What can *your client* do differently?

Describe your strengths and your operations (which is another way to say "method of delivery") from your *clients' point of view.* Why?

Because that's the only viewpoint they have. Here's a quick three-step summary:

1. Impact is seen in outcomes and in action, from the client's point of view.

2. If your client doesn't see something, it doesn't exist.

3. Speak your clients' language. Stop trying to teach them yours.

Consider these outcomes as possibilities for answering this question, *How is the client better off?*:

- More efficient ⇒ Save time

- Less downtime, fewer insurance claims, stop online security threats ⇒ Reduce risk

- Less downtime, fewer insurance claims, stop online security threats ⇒ Reduce risk ⇒ Save money ⇒ Increase peace of mind

- Promote team members, give out bonuses at the end of the year ⇒ Team members are able to put their kids in private school, save for retirement, take their grandkids to Alaska, etc. ⇒ Freedom, options, and more choices

- Help our clients to be more efficient ⇒ Our clients grow their market share

- High-quality equipment ⇒ client can assemble products more quickly and serve their market more efficiently ⇒ client's profits increase

Things like "we become more efficient" are a version of "save money," right? Because efficiency goes straight to the bottom line— *saving money.* Reaching more clients, gaining market share, increasing sales in any way. Those things point to top-line revenue growth.

Efficiency also saves the most precious resource of all: time. You can always make more money, but you can't make more time.

Look in the direction of money, time, and risk. Look at peace of mind. Look at the things we all want. Phrase your ideas from the client's point of view. Consider:

- How are you helping your team members to prosper?
- How are you helping your external clients to grow their businesses?
- How are you improving the quality of life for those you serve?
- What are you doing to help people on their path to prosperity? Do you offer challenging work, expanding learning opportunities, career mapping and mentoring?

If you want to see the result, look at what people *have* and what they can *do differently*, as a result of your *impact*.

Now, here's the biggest question of all.

Looking at your three columns once again: Which of these three columns is most important *to your client*?

1. My Greatest Strengths	2. My Method of Delivery (Transfer)	3. How Is Your Client Better Off?

The answer is always column three.

Wherever you are in your leadership journey, doing the right things means serving others. That's a language we all need to understand.

Personalizing what you have to offer and framing your operations around those you serve is the job of every leader—no matter your title, role, or responsibility.

The language and actions that you choose will define your results, building the connections that you seek, and moving your ideas and goals forward. Consider carefully the language that you use, but more importantly, ask yourself this leadership question:

How's your client doing?

Your ability to see what others need, and then deliver it, is how your strengths will come to life and how others will follow your lead.

Consider this factor of leadership.

Leadership Factor 1

The leadership conversation always starts with what your client is thinking.

Your strengths are important. Delivering your strengths is important.

But your client's viewpoint is most important of all.

The people you wish to persuade and influence are not contemplating your strengths. They are not debating whether you are an "organizer" or an "activator."

I was working with a business owner, and I asked him what made his business so successful.

"Well," he said proudly, "our engineering team has over 75 years of combined experience in our industry."

And I said, "So what?"

He looked at me for a second. Then he came at me again: "You don't understand. We were just voted one of the Best Places to Work in our metro area. For companies our size, we are the best of the best!"

And I said, "So what?"

He squinted: "Look! We have a pristine list of Fortune 1000 clients. We work with companies that are hundreds of times larger than we are, and they all love us!"

You know what I said by now. "So what?"

This CEO glares at me. "I see what you are doing. Everything I say makes you say 'so what?' But let me ask you a question," he said, gaining steam. "Just where do you get off saying 'so what' about my business?"

I stood up and looked him in the eye. "I'll tell you where I get off," I said, hitching up my britches ever so slightly. "*I'm the U.S. National Elevator Pitch Champion.*"

And he said, "So what?"

The point of the story is this: If your accomplishments, accolades, and experience don't matter to your listener, *they don't matter.* Whatever you've built, created, or developed, it doesn't exist if your *client* doesn't see it.

Want to have greater impact as a leader? Frame the conversation around what your clients want and need. See your accomplishments as a gateway to their results, and you will gain their attention. You will go from "So what?" to "Tell me more."

As I said in *The NEW Elevator Pitch,* "Tell me more" is the key to the conversation.

Don't just focus on your story. Don't puke features, numbers, data, benefits, or your experience at someone. Don't get lost on differences—your age, your tattoos, or your preference for Twitter over Instagram. There's a bigger game here.

Focus on your outcomes, phrased in terms of your most important person: your client.

How you deliver your skills is important. But your clients don't care how you make the sausage. Or deliver it. Not yet. There's one thing they want to know first:

Your clients want to know how you are going to put your strengths to work for them.

As we look at the words and actions that will help you most, you have to consider those you serve. Meet your clients where *they* are.

That conversation is where real leadership begins.

Takeaways

- The people you serve, the people you care about, the people who are the key to your success: Consider these people your *clients.*

- The strongest conversation always starts with what your client is thinking.

- Concepts like "passion" and "honesty" are important. But putting concepts into action for the clients you serve is the path to creating real impact.

- Who do you identify as your clients?

- When you look at your clients, internal or external, are you able to see a situation from their point of view? What's the value in seeing that position?

- What can you do, right now, to let your clients know how you are going to put your strengths to work . . . *for them*?

4 Conquering Change

"They always say time changes things. But actually, you have to change them yourself."

—Andy Warhol, artist and pop-culture icon

"You didn't come this far only to come this far."

—Anonymous

In general terms, which do you prefer:

Something that's new, or

Something that's familiar?

Your answer may change, depending on the circumstances. For example, when it comes to spouses and partners, most people prefer what's familiar. Until the day that they don't. Then they prefer what's new. Whether that creates problems, or freedoms, really depends on your point of view.

Sometimes we prefer the newest technology. Sometimes we prefer the more familiar apps and platforms. Have you ever bought a car in the first year the model was introduced? Or have you had the same car for the last nine years, and you hope it never dies?

Most of the time, I prefer what's new. That's just me. But even so, there are always times when the familiar is the first choice.

Even for the extreme sports enthusiast who is always looking for a new place to bungee jump, that search for a thrill is a *familiar* search. So, too, for the person who prefers the familiar: sometimes, even at your favorite restaurant, you will try an appetizer or dessert that you've never had before. You may go on vacation at the same time every year, but you go to a different destination or stay at a new hotel.

Take a look at the diagram of human nature in Figure 4.1.

We all enjoy a combination of what's known and what's new, depending on our circumstances, mood, and situation.

When you consider any leadership initiative, which side is it on? For example:

- You want your R&D team to develop and deliver a product on time and on budget, 90 days from now—and they've missed their last two milestone deadlines.

- You want your boyfriend to go on vacation with you to Maui (you've been there, but he never has).

- You are going to restructure your team in accounting and out-source some noncritical functions to a firm in Los Angeles.

Where do these leadership initiatives live? Something new, or something familiar?

Figure 4.1 The Balance Inside All of Us, Between What's New and What's Known

While it's true that these scenarios include elements of what's known (such as the R&D process, your existing team of employees, your knowledge of your boyfriend's tastes, and your understanding of accounting), leadership initiatives always consist of *what's new*. Ultimately, any change to the status quo is about something *new*.

Why? Because leadership is about change. Helping your clients to create something new, something that hasn't happened before, is the reason we need leaders. Leaders like you.

How do you find the place that challenges the status quo? It's part of the Leadership Factor.

Leadership Factor 2

To get to something new, start with something known.

While some say that familiarity breeds contempt, for the visionary leader it actually breeds acceptance. You know it to be true from your own experience. Each of us, according to our various tolerances for risk, balances novelty and familiarity when faced with any decision.

In *Impossible to Ignore*, Carmen Simon talks about the role of memory (the familiar) in creating new outcomes:

> What if memory has evolved to keep track of the future, not the past? After all, there is little evolutionary advantage for humans simply to recall the past. The advantage of remembering the past comes from using it to . . . predict and prepare for what happens next.

She goes on to summarize the relationship between familiarity and novelty:

> Remembering the past becomes useful if it gives us insight into future outcomes.

When clients come to me and tell me that they want to go on *Shark Tank*, I'm always intrigued. But if they say, "I've got an idea that's so innovative nobody's ever heard of it before!" that's a showstopper.

Time to back up the truck, Gunga Din.

Because the first step in communicating your idea now becomes one of creating familiarity where (supposedly) none exists! If you have to convince people that a warp drive is real or that a transporter beam is something that they really could use, your communication is doubly difficult.

Common connections lead to uncommon results.

We move forward from where we are *now*. Leaders see the now. And leaders see the possibilities. Leaders share their visions and their paths forward—and help others to get there.

As you will see in other chapters, framing the conversation is crucial to creating the connection you want. If there's no frame of reference, your ideas may fall on deaf ears. Why? Because the known shapes our perceptions on a constant basis.

Let's look at the relationship between the known and the unknown. Consider, for example, a simple meeting between you and your senior staff. The meeting is scheduled for Wednesday at 9 a.m. Being a diligent and logical planner, you (or your assistant) send out the meeting request and an agenda in advance.

Wednesday arrives. And here's what happens:

- You have a flat tire on the Dan Ryan expressway on your way to work.

- You can't change the tire yourself. A steady stream of oncoming traffic means you can't safely get to the tire to change it.

- You have a service for your vehicle, but they show up 30 minutes late, which makes you . . .

- . . . 30 minutes late.

- And the meeting never happens.

Sound familiar? It does for me. Especially that Dan Ryan Express-way reference. When I was in Chicago on a business trip, I had a flat tire. Like an idiot, I changed it myself, with cars whizzing by my hindquarters at 80 miles per hour . . . in the middle of winter. It was probably one of the dumbest things I've ever done. Luckily, I survived in spite of my stupidity. Which is also the title of my autobiography.

But, I digress. The point of the story is: Uncertainty is everywhere.

We put events on the calendar. We craft our well-thought-out agendas. And then someone can't make the meeting. The drawings don't arrive from the architecture firm. The real estate contract is delayed because of an unforeseen legal matter.

The idea that your life is scripted is a myth. Leaders don't believe in myths. Here's the truth: Leadership isn't scripted.

We gather data and feed our calendars so that we can remember that we don't have to worry about the things that are written down. Our calendars give us piece of mind, just like many other reports and data that I'm sure you receive in some form or another.

But life exists outside of the data. Even the most well-thought-out agenda is really just a starting point for improvisation. Working to minimize that improvisation can be an important skill. But leaders need to know how to take life as it comes—not as it appears on the calendar.

When I was younger, I did quite a bit of work on stage. I trained as an actor from my teenage years, when I was a student at Chicago's high school for the performing arts. I went on to study theater in college and earned my BFA from Southern Methodist University in Dallas. For many years, I worked as a performer on stage and in front of the camera.

I draw on this experience in my coaching and my keynotes, as you can imagine. And sometimes I help my clients to go in front of the media to tell their stories.

If there's one thing I learned about studying scripts, it's this: When it comes time to perform, the script is really just a guideline. What you think you have and what actually happens can be two wildly different things.

I'll never forget the time I was standing on stage, with my "father" in a show. He was in the middle of a speech he had given to me at least a dozen times. The theater was packed, and the audience hung on his every word. Suddenly, his face went blank.

He looked left. He looked down at the stage. Then he looked right at me. His pause had gone from dramatic to awkward, and it was getting worse by the second.

"Son," he said, with emphasis, "what was I saying?"

Welcome to improv class.

Or the time I had to deliver the "big reveal" at the end of *City of Angels*, a jazz musical wrapped around a detective story. I played a small but pivotal role. I had to deliver the huge plot twist in the final scene of the show—unmixing the mix-up that helped the detective to solve the mystery.

As directed, I came running onstage. The setup was unusual. I entered from the audience. I ran down one of the aisles in the theater onto a ramp that led to the stage. At full gallop (very dramatic!) I raced up the ramp. Not sure where I was looking—or what I was thinking—but in my haste I clipped a set piece with my shoulder, a prop of a picture window that was about 15 feet tall.

I tripped and fell like a cowboy's horse that just caught a bullet. I saw the fake window tip, spin, and follow me onto the stage—coming straight for my head! Thinking quickly, I rolled out of the way and avoided becoming a stage sandwich.

The audience was shocked. Stunned. Silent.

I managed to quickly get up. Fortunately, I wasn't hurt. I looked at the set piece. I looked at the other actors on stage.

"Do NOT," I shouted, "ask me to do that again!"

The illusion that life is planned is a fragile one. The universe continues to show me every day that discovery is the norm, not the exception, no matter how hard I try to fight it.

Perhaps you have those on your team who long for the status quo—to make sure that what got you here is where you're going to be tomorrow. "Stick to the script" is only a guideline for a leader, not a hard-and-fast rule, especially when the script is one you're writing as you go along.

The fact is that nothing stays the same. Change is all around us.

Your team may tell you that they are afraid of change. In fact, you may say that to yourself. But discomfort and uncertainty don't have to go together.

As a leader, you have to face the facts. The unexpected can show up at any time. Because it's already here. It's all around you. The good news is that you—as a human being—are wired to improvise, adapt, and overcome changing circumstances. That's true for you as a leader, and that's true for every one of your clients.

You've consistently navigated through change throughout your whole life. Adaptability is built into each of us.

Remember when you were a baby, crawling on the floor? OK, maybe you don't have that memory. But you do admit that, like everyone else on the planet, you crawled on the floor, right?

Then one day, you found yourself next to the leg of a sturdy chair. In that moment, you saw opportunity. You made an executive decision. You decided to pull yourself up.

In an instant, crawling was old news. It was time to take a stand. In that moment, you stood up. And immediately, nothing was ever going to be the same again. You were done with crawling around.

It was a simple moment of transformation. A moment when you left the past behind. That simple change meant that there was no going back. You were walking, headed toward running, and who knows what else. It all came from that moment of realization and discovery of new possibilities.

Whether you realize it or not, you've been repeating this process throughout your life.

- There was a time when you had never driven a car, and then you did.
- There was a time when you had never visited the college that you attended, and then you did.
- There was a time when you had never eaten sushi, and then you did.
- There was a time when you had never been a part of the C-Suite, and then you were.

You may work for an organization that has never made more than $50 million in revenues. And then, one day . . . guess what? That threshold is reached. And exceeded.

Companies and individuals reach unexpected milestones every day.

Are you ready to lead yourself and your team into that brave new world? Are you ready to pull yourself up and walk forward toward the possibilities? Life is a dizzying combination of what's new, and what's known.

Here's what this means to you as a leader:

- **Change Doesn't Stop You.** Everyone faces change every day, even under the most mundane and commonplace circumstances. People work hard to "keep their heads down" and "plan ahead" to minimize the unknown and the risks associated with new circumstances. But what's new doesn't have to be what's stopping you . . . or your team. See past the myth of change: you have conquered massive changes in your life, time and time again. And that's true for every one of your team members, your clients, and all those you serve.

- **Discomfort and uncertainty don't have to go together.** You may be uncertain about what you're going to have for lunch next Tuesday. But you also know that you will figure it out when it's time to get something to eat! What's the big deal? Well, what happens when you realize that you're going to figure out whatever it is that looks impossible to you right now? That's not motivational mumbo jumbo. That's the way things work! When your worrying settles down, new ideas can show up. A baby doesn't contemplate whether walking is a possibility. A baby grabs the leg of the chair and keeps moving forward! Maybe a little bit of action is what is needed. Don't let the unknown stop you.

- **Why "No" isn't the final answer.** Look closely at what appears to be an impossible problem right now. When I work with my coaching clients, we often discover that there's a nearby chair leg . . . and it's closer than you might think. When asked about change, a client might answer, "No! I don't want to change and neither does my team!" Even though that change might be inevitable, it's seldom desirable—at least, when we are fearful of the newness of it all. Have you ever noticed how much energy it takes to resist something? Instead of fighting for a past that doesn't serve you, remember the words from scientist Roger von Oech: "Always look for the second right answer."

- **That answer—the one that helps you adapt to change—is on its way.** If it weren't, you'd still be crawling around on the floor!

Takeaways

- Uncertainty and discomfort don't have to go together. Leaders embrace change and help others to do the same, because they know how things work.

- Look for places where you are resisting the thing that's useful, powerful, and helpful. Look at the places where you are resisting the way things work. Is that useful, powerful, and helpful? Or exhausting?

- We all have the ability to improvise, adapt, and overcome. That's not to say that leadership is about going "off script." Instead, it's about knowing that you are wired to deal with the unexpected. Can you think of a time when life was unscripted and unexpected? How did you react?

- In the face of uncertainty, what changes for you when you understand that you have a lifelong history of overcoming your circumstances? When you consider that you've been creating powerful change (a change that means you never do something the same way again) since you were wearing diapers? If you're wearing underwear right now, you've made the change I'm talking about. And if you're reading this chapter in the nude, well, what can I tell ya? That's exactly how I wrote it. So we are pretty much twinsies, aren't we?

Resource

von Oech, Roger. *A Whack on the Side of the Head: How You Can Be More Creative* (rev. ed.). New York: Warner Books, 2008.

5 Influence and the Empty Chair

"The world is more malleable than you think and it's waiting for you to hammer it into shape."

—Bono, lead singer of U2

"The greatest mistake you can make in life is continually fearing you will make one."

—Elbert Hubbard, writer

My friend Jason was the CEO of a publicly traded consumer finance company. We'd known each other since college. The company had 6,000 employees. Over coffee, I asked him what it was like to sit in the Captain's Chair.

"It's not easy," he shared, "being responsible for over 14,000 people."

Wait a minute. That math doesn't make sense. Jason was a former CFO, he ran a finance company, and it looked like he had his numbers wrong! Did he mean 14,000 shareholders or something?

What was I missing?

"I'm taking the average family size of 2.3 kids and multiplying it by all my employees," he explained. "Some may not have children, some may have four or five. It's an estimate. The point is: I consider the people this company supports, because that's who my employees are considering, right now."

That was the way he looked at his leadership responsibility. How do you see yours?

Consider, for a moment, an empty chair.

In the leadership conversation, the empty chair is always an available seat at the table. It's a metaphorical seat, for someone who's going to be dramatically and personally impacted by the change that you propose. However, that "someone" isn't in the room when you propose your change. Your ideas. Your vision.

And yet, that person is the one who will be dramatically and personally impacted by your leadership language. Because all persuasive conversations are, at their core, about change.

Here are two examples:

1. The empty chair is a seat at the table for the third-grade student in McAllen, Texas. She's not in the room when the teachers and school administrators are deciding which history textbook to use. In fact, if she were there, she couldn't really advocate for her own interests. She couldn't say which textbook would be best. But she will be directly and dramatically impacted by the change that they propose. That history book will help her come to understand the world around her, exploring ideas from beyond the Rio Grande Valley as she comes to understand the past.

2. The empty chair is a seat at the table for the patient who is going to go through the MRI machine. He's not in the room when the doctors and hospital administrators are making that seven-figure investment decision. And yet, directly, personally, and powerfully impacted, when that machine provides a diagnosis that could save his life.

The empty chair points to an important aspect of human nature: We are all thinking of the exact same thing, right now:

We are all thinking about ourselves.

That's not to say that you are selfish, or that I am selfish. No. What I'm saying is that we are all wired to think and act in our own self-interests.

Scientists call this our "survival instinct," and it's a part of the fabric of every human mind. Some would point out that our focus on ourselves is part of our lizard brain or limbic brain—the primitive part of ourselves that's focused on survival.

But, beyond thinking like a lizard, we all share another common characteristic. Right now, as I write these words, I have people who are here with me . . . but they are not literally "here with me." I'm talking about my family, my business partners, my clients, my team at Wiley. I carry these folks with me wherever I go.

Do you have anyone who's "here with you" in your mind, even if he or she is not physically with you right now? That's the person who sits in your empty chair.

The empty chair is a seat that's reserved for the person (or people) you care about most. True, we are all focused on our own self-interests. But those interests always extend outward to the people that you and I care about the most.

If I have someone who sits in the empty chair, and you have someone who sits in the empty chair, then perhaps we are looking at an aspect of human nature. Maybe we are taking a peak into the universal aspect of how we all work. It's a universal principle that gives insight into the power of acknowledgment, if you choose to look in that direction.

At a fundamental level, leadership is about influence. Not titles. Not salaries. *Influence.*

Consider those whom you wish to influence and persuade. The people you wish to influence are people of great importance. You could say that the person you wish to persuade is your client, your most important person.

So follow the logic: Your client's client sits in the empty chair.

Leadership Factor 3

Your client's client sits in the empty chair.

When you get right down to it, your client is your most important person.

In a workshop, I had someone ask, "So is my wife my client?"

My reply: "I sure hope so." And I hope that's how you feel about your husband as well.

Leaders: take care of your clients, or someone else will.

If you want to gain real insight into those you serve, and those you wish to influence, acknowledge those you serve and those who serve you. Consider this question:

Who sits in the empty chair?

- For yourself?
- For your CFO?
- For your boss?
- For your board of directors?
- For your largest client?
- For a client you haven't met yet?

As a leader, recognition is a powerful tool. Being able to sincerely say, "I see you," can be a powerful way to start the conversation. If your position or title inspires others to follow your ideas, looking at their wants and needs can be a source of authentic influence and connection. Simply acknowledge our human nature—acknowledge the empty chair—and you will see beyond recognition to the things that matter most.

Leaders recognize the power of acknowledgment. That acknowledgment rises to a new level when you consider the empty chair. The empty chair allows you to say, "Not only do I see you, but I see what—and *who*—really matters to you."

When you think about creating real influence, think about the empty chair. Because your client always is.

Takeaways

- Connection isn't something to strive for: It's something to be observed.

- We all share common characteristics, wants, and needs. Noticing what brings us together can help leaders to bring others to a common goal.

- That connection is right here, right now, if you are willing to see it. How can you share what we all have in common as a way to create uncommon results?

- Who sits in the empty chair for you?

- How important is family when it comes to what motivates you? How does that translate for the people you work with every day?

- Can you see how an idea or objective could sit in the empty chair? For example, could increasing the company's profit margin, or painlessly removing the old software system, or improving video views on YouTube, be top of mind for your client?

6 Discovering Your Leadership Vision

"A vision's just a vision if it's only in your head. If no one gets to see it, it's as good as dead."

—Excerpted from *Sunday in the Park with George*
by Stephen Sondheim

Did you know that it's physically impossible to hit a major league fastball?

According to Yale physicist, Robert Adair, every major league batter is faced with an impossible problem. Adair was the "physicist to the National League" in the late 1980s. In his book, *The Physics of Baseball*, he shows that the numbers don't add up when it's time to put the bat on the ball.

For a major league fastball, traveling at over 90 miles per hour, it takes just 400 milliseconds to travel from the pitcher's hand to the catcher's mitt. The pitcher's mound is 60 feet, six inches, from home plate, but you have to factor in the length of the pitcher's stride to really gauge the pitch.

- The human eye requires nearly 100 milliseconds just to process the image of the ball.
- From the brain to the muscles, the impulse to swing takes another 25 milliseconds.

- The actual swing itself requires 150 milliseconds, as the bat speed goes from 0 to over 70 mph on the way to making contact with the ball

- That means a batter has—at best—just 125 milliseconds to assess the pitch and decide whether to go for it.

For comparison: it takes 300 to 400 milliseconds just to blink.

"You can't think and hit at the same time."

—YOGI BERRA

There isn't enough time for a batter to accurately gauge a pitch, time his swing, and make contact with the ball. Our minds can't process information quickly enough. And these scientific facts make Stanley Anderson a superhero.

Stanley Anderson isn't a major league baseball player. He's a 56-year-old security guard from Detroit, Michigan. And he can hit a 266 mph fastball.

A baseball enthusiast who never played in the big leagues, Anderson always enjoyed going to the batting cages. Anderson explains that he started moving out "past the red line" until he was just 17 feet away from the pitching machine. Seventeen feet!

- At that distance, the speed of a pitch is the equivalent of 266 miles per hour.

- At that distance, Anderson has just 180 milliseconds to connect with the ball! (Compare that to the time required to hit a major league fastball.)

- At that distance, he faced off against 22,750 pitches in 2016. He failed to make contact with the ball just 98 times!

What makes Anderson able to accomplish the impossible? The answer may surprise you: *anticipation.*

We all have the ability to ANTICIPATE. Anticipation is what makes the connection possible. That's true on the baseball field, and it's true in the leadership conversation. It just so happens that Mr. Anderson is better at it than most.

Beyond the batter's box, something more than physical attributes makes the impossible possible, even for regular folks like you and me.

Anticipation is a super-power we all share.

In other words, the ability to see outcomes, even in the face of incomplete information. *Anticipation* is what makes up for a lack in vision.

If we couldn't anticipate, we could never turn left into traffic. We could never envision new business opportunities, never create a work of art or new software, or … anything, really!

That's why you have to understand how to leverage your natural ability—the ability to anticipate—to create your leadership vision. Your leadership vision is based, in part, on anticipation.

When you look in the direction of your clients—those who you serve—what do you see? What is it that you *anticipate*? Perhaps more importantly, what is your *client* anticipating, right now? Things like:

- On-time delivery
- Products that don't break
- A trustworthy boss who's watching out for the interests of employees and shareholders with equal fairness
- A company that understands the requirements of corporate social responsibility
- A service representative who doesn't avoid the tough conversations and knows how to deliver the news (even when it's bad)

What else?

Baseball is a game of deception, from the pitcher's mound to the batter's box. Pitchers work hard to make sure you don't see what's coming. But as leaders, you want to be transparent, visible, and clear to those on your team. You anticipate their needs. You make it easy for your clients to see where you're coming from.

When you combine your vision, and your ability to anticipate, you discover the four words that are the foundation of *Leadership Language*. For yourself, your team, your ideas, and your initiatives, these four words—and your ability to bring them to life—are central to your impact as a leader. Here they are:

I've thought this through.

Leaders see the parts, but ultimately, leadership language focuses on the whole. And not just the whole picture, but the *impact* of the whole picture. Thinking things through doesn't mean that you focus intently on the 76 steps in your planning process. Actually, quite the opposite. Thinking things through is a reminder to look past the nose on your face.

Thinking things through means that you look in the direction of outcomes and results, not just processes. Planning is important, but look beyond your plan if you want to see where influence really comes from. Consider the *ripple effect.*

The ripple effect of your vision is also called "impact." If you are lost in your plans and your well-thought-out agenda, you are just lost. Thinking things through means thinking not just about yourself or your calendar but also how your client is doing.

Thinking things through means considering the impact of your actions. The six steps in your plan are not as important as the one outcome you hope to create. Because sometimes, step number four becomes step number one. What do you do when life throws you a change-up? How you react is more important than checking off boxes and following your punch list.

You want to win. If you didn't, you probably wouldn't be reading this book. There's one thing that's more important than tips, techniques, and strategies when it comes to winning.

That one thing? *Understanding.*

Understanding means empathy. Understanding means emotional intelligence. Understanding means knowing the implications of your actions. Understanding how things work allows you to think things through in a powerful way. Because you see things that others don't. Or won't. Or can't.

Your understanding is where your vision is leading you. *Leadership Language* is about sharing that understanding with others.

- What is it, right now, that your team doesn't understand?
- What is it, right now, that you don't understand about your team?

A leader looks for those answers. A leader has the courage to listen when those answers show up. A leader understands the physics and engineering behind a new kind of conversation. Physics helps us to see beyond myths and mysteries. Physics is how things really work. Engineering is how you can make things work for you. And for your clients. Figure 6.1 shows how these various pieces of leadership fit together.

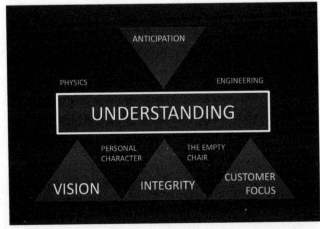

Figure 6.1 Understanding Is the Basis of *Leadership Language*

Here's an exercise that I've used with my technology clients, and it's helpful in determining your vision—for yourself and for your organization.

You have to become a Traveler.

A traveler, in this case, refers to the wildly inventive Netflix series, *Travelers.* Produced by Eric McCormack of *Will & Grace* fame, the show features McCormack as a time traveler from the future who, through the magic of science fiction, literally takes over the body and life of a twenty-first-century FBI agent. Guided by a sophisticated AI from the future, McCormack and his team have traveled back in time to rewrite history—hoping to avoid the apocalyptic future that started their time travel in the first place.

You don't have to lead a team back in time to become a Traveler. All you have to do is write an email … to yourself. But here's the catch: in order to make it work, this email comes from your future self. In fact, 12 months in the future. In your email, you write back to yourself. You write what you've accomplished and achieved over the past year. You fast-forward yourself in your imagination and look back.

Perhaps you touch on the challenges you've faced over the past year. What did you overcome? How did you do it? What's gone from your life? And what remains?

Your leadership time travel could show you some things you haven't considered:

- What does your Traveler have to say about the vision you've created?

- What is it that your future self would say created the biggest "Wow" over the past year?

Remember, there's no right or wrong answer. And there's no reason why you can't write more than one email. If small, incremental improvements represent a big victory for you, that's fine. But I wonder: Is that all there is?

The Travelers came back to rewrite history. To change the events that shaped the future. What future are you shaping in your Traveler email? Dream big!

However, if 0.034 percent growth is exciting to you, I don't want to rob you of your enthusiasm. Hey, if the last year was down by 28 percent, any positive number could be a big improvement!

But … is that all there is? Incremental growth feels like management to me. Not leadership. Leaders see possibilities where others don't see anything at all.

When you do look beyond what's gone before, what shows up? I wonder whether your Traveler will see what has to change in order for your results to change. Put that in your email!

If you want to lead others to a new vision, you first have to see that vision for yourself. I would encourage you to look beyond step-by-step improvements when it comes to your Traveler journey.

My friend Jeffrey Hayzlett wrote a great book: *Think Big, Act Bigger*. The title alone has always stuck with me. "Thinking Big" isn't about acting like a big shot or trying to be someone you're not. Big thinking isn't about big egos, if you do it right.

Think big: See the possibilities.

Act bigger: Take the biggest action you can to bring your vision to life.

When you act bigger, you are becoming *more* of yourself—more authentic about what you really want—and more aligned with the actions that can help you to realize your vision.

For me, thinking big is about permission. Permission to see what you'd like, and to truly pursue it. Transformation is right here, right now, if you give yourself permission to see it.

Transformation is never more than one thought away.

"Don't bunt. Aim out of the ballpark. Aim for the company of immortals."

—DAVID OGILVY, ADVERTISING EXECUTIVE

Takeaways

Here are seven anticipation questions that can point you in the direction of your vision. Remember, hope is not a strategy. What is the action that will influence, build, or make your vision come to life?

- Talk to your Traveler: One year from now, what has made you say, "Wow!"?

- Given what we know now, what unexpected challenge is most likely to occur?

- Given what we know now, what is the timing that can help or hinder our anticipated results?

- Given what we know now, what tools or skills could help our anticipated results?

- What's the impact, assuming we reach our goal?

- What assumptions are we using to anticipate the future? And what could change if we plugged in a new set of assumptions?

- Who could you talk to, right now, to give you a fresh perspective?

And a bonus question:

- *What else should you consider?*

Resource

Hayzlett, Jeffrey W., and Eber, Jim. *Think Big, Act Bigger: The Rewards of Being Relentless.* Irvine, CA: Entrepreneur Press, 2015

7 Are You Listening?

"Most people do not listen with the intent to understand; they listen with the intent to reply."

—Stephen R. Covey, author, *7 Habits of Highly Effective People*

"If you make listening and observation your occupation, you will gain much more than you can by talk."

—Robert Baden Powell, first chief of the Boy Scouts of America

In any conversation there are two parts: what is said and what is heard. For a leader who wishes to persuade and inspire, which part is most important?

For me, speaking nearly a hundred times a year to groups of all shapes and sizes, I've discovered that what I have to say is never as important as what people actually hear. I work hard on my content and on my delivery. When it comes time to lead and influence others, I put my attention where it really belongs: on my audience.

If you're wondering what's going through my head before I step on stage for a keynote or workshop, the answer is: as little as possible.

I have found that when my thinking quiets down, I can really listen—really engage with the people who matter most. That may sound weird, since I'm the one doing most of the talking in my keynote. But I also need to listen to myself.

I've learned what you already know: I can listen while I'm speaking. You can too—and you already do it. Every time you engage in a conversation, presentation, or meeting, your eyes are open (whether your mouth is or not). Your powers of observation are always available. *You can listen with your eyes.*

But please don't use that as your headline on your LinkedIn profile. Or on match.com.

Here's the point: You may not directly ask for feedback. Your client may not be talking. But there are nonverbal clues all around you. Observe the clues.

Leadership Factor 4

Leaders listen with their eyes as well as their ears.

The CEO was on edge. His business development guy had only been with the company for six months. Somehow, the "New Guy" had managed to get an audience with the general manager and forty of his senior staff at the world-renown Bellagio Hotel in Las Vegas. The conversation centered on an innovative new technology product, designed for the luxury hotel market—a market that, until now, was largely underserved by the company. Somehow, New Guy had landed a meeting to talk about the platform the company had developed. The CEO smelled risk—and exposure: What if this presentation didn't go well?

Sitting at the back of the room, the seasoned executive perched on the edge of his seat. Sure, he realized that the New Guy was the product expert. But New Guy was an unknown quantity! The CEO leaned over to his second in command—Scott Norder—and nudged him.

"You've got to get in there!" he whispered. "You've got to get in front of these people and nail this presentation!"

Norder was one of the C-suite leaders at the company, and he knew the value of patience. A former engineer from Chicago, he was one of the key spokespeople at the company, often commenting on analyst calls and speaking at industry events.

"The New Guy has got this," Norder whispered back. "Wait. Just wait. If I need to jump in, I will. *But I don't.*"

Have you ever been there, as an executive supporting a major purchase decision, and you've had to bite your tongue? It's not easy! Norder was a trusted advisor to the CEO. His word was his bond. Together, on his recommendation, the two senior leaders kept silent.

The New Guy was allowed to run the meeting—a meeting he had set up that featured the technology he had helped to develop. Instead of rushing in, the leaders gave something more valuable: they gave an *opportunity* to the New Guy. And, by extension, they gave that opportunity to the leadership team at Bellagio.

Norder knew the content. He knew the New Guy. He knew that the story would unfold without interference. And if interference was necessary, a senior leader was standing by, patiently ready to engage, but wisely avoiding the impulse to interfere. To micromanage. To disrupt the plan before it unfolded completely.

> *"Few things can help an individual more than to place responsibility on him, and to let him know that you trust him."*
>
> —BOOKER T. WASHINGTON, EDUCATOR AND FOUNDER OF
> TUSKEGEE UNIVERSITY

The New Guy had no idea of the conversation at the back of the room. He was oblivious to the heated dialogue, suspicion, and staccato whispers that could have derailed the presentation. But they didn't. And the New Guy was forever grateful.

The New Guy went on to place innovative new products at a variety of hotels across North America and, later, around the world.

In the process, he learned a valuable leadership lesson: Leaders allow others to do their jobs.

I can tell you personally that the New Guy has never forgotten that lesson. Because I was that New Guy.

When my boss, Scott Norder, and the CEO, Bob Carroll, told me about the debate that raged in the back of the room, I was stunned. The trust they gave me in Las Vegas was a priceless gift—a gift that I pay forward every day. "How exactly," Bob asked over dinner, "did you get this meeting?"

"I called them and asked for it," I said sheepishly. Was that a big deal? The New Guy was too dumb to know better, I guess.

I went on to build and lead teams around the world, and the hotel business formed the basis of the company's valuation, which led my publicly traded employer to be sold into the private sector at a nice multiplier on earnings.

As the business development executive in charge of the hotel business, the products we introduced that day at Bellagio were later sold to multiple MGM Mirage properties, Caesars Palace, and many other hotels up and down the strip. I had the opportunity to work with some of the world's largest lodging companies, from New York to L.A., later building a team to focus on the residential business across the entire nation.

But ultimately, that day at Bellagio wasn't about market impact, revenue, or future valuations. The real results didn't come from my presentation skills.

Trust is the real hero of this story.

Trust allowed these leaders to *listen*, instead of rushing in—where their input would have done more harm than good. Why more harm? Because if they mistrusted me, *so would the client*. That's what Bob Carroll knew, and that's why he listened. Bob was one of the best CEOs I have ever met—his ability to allow others to do what they do best was his superpower. I was grateful for the trust he gave me on that day in Las Vegas, and on many days after that.

The ability to listen is key to your success. Listening is about *observation*—taking in the language (and body language) of those around you. In this listening context, it can be useful to set the stage for a new kind of conversation. In my workshops with executives and executive teams, we often focus on how to really hear and engage with what others are saying.

It takes confidence and courage to set aside your infatuation with your own message and engage with someone else's story. But how can we learn and grow if we can't access another perspective?

Remember: None of us is as smart as all of us.

Do you know how to truly listen and observe?

When team leaders understand how to hear things differently, the conversation changes.

Does listening really matter? Think about a time when you were really heard, listened to, and understood.

- Who were you with?
- How did you feel?
- When did you know that you were being heard?
- What did you see and hear that was previously hidden? What did you uncover in that conversation?
- What changed for you during that conversation?
- What was the impact of someone really listening to your ideas?

The ability to engage and listen opens up the conversation, allowing others to reveal that which was previously unseen. However, you have to make sure that you are looking in the same direction and providing space for that kind of conversation.

Three Ways to Listen

It seems that there are really three ways to listen. The first way is to *listen to affirm*. You are finding the relationships between what you already know and what you are hearing. You may experience "listening to affirm" as you read this book, if you find yourself making comparisons to other authors you have read.

And people are doing the same thing when you share your vision. They're comparing you to the previous CEO or to what they read in a book by John Maxwell, or perhaps Tim Ferriss.

But references and comparisons can take you out of the conversation. If you're making comparisons to someone else, how are you really able to be present and engage with the person right in front of you?

The second way to listen is to *listen to defend*. That's how lawyers listen. By taking a defensive posture, your focus shifts to your response. Stephen Covey describes it like this: listening is merely a delay in your ability to respond. Essentially, you only listen well enough to counterpunch. Your attention is on yourself. Focusing on your own story and how to defend it dismisses what the other person has to say. It's how you politely listen to someone tell you about his or her vacation, just so you can say, "Well, when *we* went to Monterrey last spring...."

Dismissal, in this case, is disagreement. That disagreement closes off the realm of possibility. Why? Because, no matter what the possibilities are, your disagreement will cause you to miss them.

The third way to listen—and this is the way that is most valuable—is to *listen to discover*. And it's the hardest thing for a leader to do.

Why?

Because *listening to discover* isn't about you.

Listening to discover will point you in the direction of innovation. New results. New collaboration. Listening to discover will show you what's missing. For yourself, and for your client. Are you in love with what you already know? Is your expertise so beautiful and compelling that you can't look away from your own experience or stop talking about it?

If you think you have to go it alone and your story is the only one that matters, I need you to discover something right now: You misunderstand about what really matters.

If you're unable to listen to discover, how are you going to change the game? How are you going to lead others to new outcomes if you won't engage in the place where those outcomes live? *Discover that place.* Let go of the misunderstanding that your voice and your affirmations are what matter most. Because they don't—and there's nothing for you to defend either. Your expertise isn't diminished, it's enhanced, because you can discover the insights you need, for the results you want.

We all listen to affirm ("I'll wait until she says something that confirms what I already know, so I can feel good about myself, my education level, my experience, etc."). Note that working hard to prove your intelligence isn't going to expand it.

And we all listen to defend ("I can't wait to tell Pat why this idea is idiotic/I've got to fix this clown/Will she ever shut up?"). You get the idea. That's how lawyers listen: trying to find the angles and the rebuttal before it's too late.

Consider some of your recent listening experiences:

- What kind of listening showed up in your last meeting?
- Who was listening to defend, and who was listening to affirm?
- And who was just checking text messages?
- When you talk to your boyfriend, spouse, or partner, how do you listen? And how do they?

We know, as leaders, that there are always things to discover.

Innovation doesn't come from what you already know.

And listening to discover is the first step toward seeing things in a new way.

Today, our ability to listen is under attack. We are bombarded by millions of messages every day. Tweets and texts and YouTube videos all compete for your attention. You're familiar with the statistic: The average attention span of an adult, right now, is eight seconds. Compare that to the average attention span of a goldfish, which is nine seconds.

If you're wondering how I know that's a fact, it's because I *read it on the Internet.*

Looking beyond our shrinking attention spans, you will see something that is quite expansive. Something that a leader can and must use to build the connections that matter most:

- Your team members, your boss, your shareholders all want to know whether you are really listening. Are you really watching, hearing, and acting on what's going on around you?

- If you are listening to affirm or to defend, whose agenda are you on?

- When you say, "I hear your concerns," do people believe you?

It's vital that you take in and acknowledge diverse points of view. However, acknowledgment is not the same as agreement. Your strength as a leader comes from understanding. Seeing another point of view doesn't mean you agree with it. It means you see it, fully. You don't need shortcuts or impatience if they don't serve you. How often do you find yourself instantly creating artificial deadlines and cutting off the conversation as a result?

Falling back into old habits or listening to discover: both options are only one thought away. The choice is yours.

Why can't you let people at least finish their thoughts?

Listening is a critical skill, because people often share the inconsequential. The conversation almost always starts with chit chat, even when the stakes are high. It takes time to get to what's really vital. Nothing's ever wrong when the conversation begins. Not because people are dishonest. It's because it takes time to find—and share—what's really going on. That's why I hate softball questions like "What keeps you up at night?" and "What are your pain points?"

Ask a high-powered executive what keeps him up at night. He'll tell you that his diamond shoes are too tight and he can't figure out where to park his jet. You know why? Because we don't like to talk about what's wrong. Not when you're sitting in the C-suite.

Do people have to be sleepless and in pain for you to help them to be better? Do your clients need to suffer first in order to want what's best? No. Not at all.

I serve a clientele that is highly effective. Some might even say that my clients are the best of the best. So why are they my clients? Because of their pain? No. Because of their desire to find more ease and grace in difficult circumstances, create greater impact, and do more stuff that makes them say, "Wow!"

Asking simple questions will not create the kind of conversation you need. Probing can be useful, but not when it's a crutch. What would you like to say if you had all your "pain point" questions answered? And what if someone isn't in pain? Can you still provide a solution that's valuable and compelling?

Leaders provide insight that shapes the conversation. Feel free to skip the language you heard in your sales training class. There's a stronger dialogue available, and it's completely pain-free. Most people almost never offer deep solutions at the outset of the conversation.

That's why "What keeps you up at night?" is a dumb question. But it can get smarter, if you follow it up with this one:

"… And what else?"

You have to make room for new ideas, knowing that people don't open with what's really on their minds. It's just human nature! Sometimes, we don't *know* what's really the source of the irritation.

Listen to this: We all need a good listener so we can talk it out!

Guide the conversation toward the discovery that hasn't shown up yet. A sense of urgency is important, but as the great UCLA basketball coach, John Wooden, said: "Be quick. But don't hurry." Give the conversation—and your client—the time to unravel new opportunities. Otherwise, your impatience will create your blind spot.

Here are four strategies to help you to listen more fully and completely:

- **Start small.** Practice giving one person your undivided attention for a small amount of time, maybe just one or two minutes. And then, really engage and listen. It's easier than you might think. Imagine this scenario: Your daughter comes to you and says, "Dad (or Mom), I've got a problem. I need your help." How would you respond? Would you say:

  - "I know exactly what it is!"
  - "Well, I've solved thousands of problems for people at work, including folks just like you!"
  - "Here, read this book. No, wait! I'll Google the answer for you, and you'll be all set!"

  I sure hope not. And so does she.

  Listen as if you were speaking to someone in your family.

  Listen as if her words will guide you, and without those words you are lost.

  Listen as if you are listening to music. You're not trying to figure out what key it's in, you're just listening—seeing where it's going—and not killing the jam with your agenda.

  Listen to discover how you can be of service.

Notice what's taking you out of the conversation. What are you worried about?

- **Shape the conversation.** Here's an idea that's especially useful if you have received less-than-stellar feedback regarding your listening skills. Let team members know that hearing them out is important. Ask whether they would help you. Ask them to consider how to compress their important ideas and conversation into a two-minute kernel, and in return, you agree to put down your phone, look away from your screen, and really explore their points of view. Do it in a one-on-one, private meeting with each of your team members.

  If you run this idea past someone and he says, "My ideas are too complex! I can't possibly describe what I want to cover in two minutes or less!," then it seems to me that he hasn't *thought this through*. What's the one big idea? What's the one key element that needs your undivided attention? It's more than fair for you to ask your team members to use their critical thinking skills and discernment before they show up and throw up with a 5,000-word treatise on why you're carrying too much inventory in the warehouse in Muncie.

  Important conversations are a two-way street. Don't be afraid to give someone a road map and expect him to follow the course. Just make sure you do your part and take the journey with him. You must sincerely want to improve your listening. So you have to come to this exercise from a place of personal growth. And if you find that the dialogue needs to go longer, then take the time. That two minutes might turn into something more.

- **Throw out your agenda.** I hate to break it to you, but nobody really cares about a well-thought-out agenda. Agendas help people to settle down so they can make plans about where not to listen. What would happen if the conversation unfolded ... naturally?

  Now, it may not be possible or practical to eliminate agendas entirely. I get that. But get this: How much detail do you really need? Agendas are just suggestions anyway. Have you ever been in a meeting where the real progress happened after the items on the agenda?

When you know what you want to discuss, and you know what you want to discover, point people in that direction. But don't dictate every twist and turn! You can use the unknown to your advantage.

Imagine that you are lost in the woods without a GPS or phone. What would be the first thing you would do? You would have to really take note of your surroundings. You would try to orient yourself, find a direction, look for clues that might lead you back to where you were. You would *listen* to your surroundings.

In the absence of an agenda, people are forced to *listen*. Look, I'm not saying that timing isn't useful. I'm not saying that you should trash any and all agendas and go freestyle in a board meeting. Put your tie on, if that's what's expected. But look beyond deadlines, and don't let them rule your world. When your agenda is perfect, your calendar wins. But do you?

- **Eliminate distractions.** Simon Sinek, author of *Start with Why* and *Leaders Eat Last*, talks about how his friends all put their cell phones into a hat before they go out for dinner or spend time at a pub. Why wouldn't you consider the same "face time" for your company meetings? Have people turn in their cell phones before the conversation begins. Put down the phone and pick up the conversation.

Roger That

Here are three phrases that can provide the acknowledgment you need, even if you know you can't agree:

- "I see what you're saying."
- "If I understand correctly, you're suggesting...."
- "I think what you are describing is...."

These phrases use "vision words" to acknowledge what you have heard. The key here is to sincerely express these words, without a lot of emotional baggage attached. These phrases are followed by an unemotional explanation of your client's point of view.

These don't work: rolling your eyes, taking a sarcastic tone, or lacing your words with mistrust when you say, "I see what you're saying. . . ." Remember, *Leadership Language* isn't just about the words you choose. Alignment and authenticity are key. Connect with your story, and with your client, if you want to be heard.

Borrow a strategy from none other than Abraham Lincoln. Lincoln was known as "honest Abe" because, as a lawyer, he would often argue opposing counsel's case in his opening remarks. He would state the facts from the other side's point of view. (Unfortunately, this level of discourse doesn't seem to be too popular in U.S. politics right now. But leadership isn't about popularity. It's about making the hard choices. And doing the right things, no matter what's trending on Twitter.) Leadership language isn't about just saying anything—it's about saying the right thing.

Until you can see and describe the other person's viewpoint, what makes you think that he or she is going to see yours? By the way, "Because I'm the boss" is never an acceptable answer. Your title might get you compliance, but that's not leadership. "Do it because I said so" is about as useful as a buggy whip, and just as outdated.

Other helpful phrases:

- **"Did I get that right?"** Here again is another way to outline what you have heard, followed by what you see as the impact of the conversation. You're not asking for anything other than confirmation. Asked and answered is the goal. If not, listen to discover what you missed!

- **"What's showing up for you right now?"** Leaders share their visions. That means checking in, from time to time, to find out what others are seeing. Are you sensing confusion, resistance, misunderstanding, or insight from your audience? Stop. Look. Listen. Are you seeing your clients or listening to your own insecurity? Leaders know the difference. Provide an opportunity for sharing and ask questions to make sure you're on track. Let your team know that you are expecting candid feedback, then show them that you have the courage to hear it.

- **"What are you *really* seeing?"** If you're not getting what you need, prompt gently for feedback, and make space so that others can express themselves. Look in the direction of "What else?"

- **"What's your biggest concern, and why is it stopping you from really saying what's on your mind?"** Leaders don't duck. How can you run your life, your career, and your business without honesty from yourself and from those you lead? If someone has concerns, better to hear them out; otherwise, you'll be fixing the wrong things, talking past the real issues, and missing the obstacles that are holding your client back.

- **"Can I ask you. . . ?"** Permission is an important part of any conversation, even when you are in charge! It may seem counter-intuitive to ask for permission, especially if you live in a country where free speech is guaranteed. But just because you *can* say something doesn't guarantee that someone will listen. Permission opens the door to a conversation, via a simple invitation to partner around an issue. Remember, until they see it, it doesn't exist. Come right at the heart of the conversation and ask the question that opens up the dialogue. For example:

  - Can I ask you to take a look at this part of your performance?

  - Can I ask you why you didn't talk to Charlie the minute you saw the parts were missing?

  - Can I ask you to take another look at the budget for next year?

Also, I do know that the proper English is "*May* I ask you . . . ?" and now you do, too. Please choose the words that feel most natural to you!

The unspoken conversation can hurt you. If you plow through your agenda without plugging in to those around you, you'll hit all your data points but miss all the potential obstacles. Instead of answering a question that no one's asked, why not stop and look for the one thing everyone needs: a chance to be heard?

What's most important in your presentation: getting through to slide 47 or getting through to the people who matter most to you? If your client is stuck on slide 46, don't leave until you know the reason why!

In the final analysis, there's one thing that's more important than the words you choose: *connection*. Connect the emotion to the passion to the vision behind the words. It's a mistake to think that words *alone* can make everything right.

Language is more than just words; there's tone, inflection, attitude, body language. In a word: connection.

There's one thing that speaks louder than words: *actions*. The action that you take is what brings your conversation to life. Are you really *connected to* what you are saying? Are you connected to your *client* as well?

Leadership Factor 5

Leaders are deeply aligned with both sides of the conversation.

Sincerity. Authenticity. Connecting. Intention. Listening. These are the actions that will speak louder than your words. If you are not sincere about asking someone's permission, asking the person to look at things in a new way, and honestly wanting to see your client's viewpoint, my voodoo will not help you.

Your words, surrounded by sincere intentions, placed in a context of listening to discover—that's where the magic can truly begin.

Takeaways

- There are no time limits on results. Be quick. But don't hurry.

- If you are plagued by distractions, eliminate them. Put down your phone and pick up the conversation.

- Asking others for what you need is the first step in finding new results. Whether it's short bursts of information or an agreement to put down cell phones during your next meeting, put your desired behaviors out there. Don't make people guess at what you really want.

- Consider how much you really care about the conversation you are having. It might be difficult to get excited about an inventory report or a marketing plan, so what is it that you've missed?

- Stop looking for a pain that you can exploit. Instead, concentrate on the solution you can provide or the one that you need from your team.

- There's something engaging in every conversation. Listen for it. Look for it. Bring it into the conversation. What can you do, right now, to recognize *connection* (connection to your subject matter and connection to your client)? What does this conversation mean to the person right in front of you?

Resources

Sinek, Simon. *Leaders Eat Last: Why Some Teams Pull Together and Others Don't.* New York: Portfolio/Penguin, 2017.

Sinek, Simon. *Start with Why: How Great Leaders Inspire Everyone to Take Action.* New York: Portfolio/Penguin, 2011.

8 The Surprise Inside

"Listen to the voice inside your head that says, 'you cannot paint,' then by all means paint, and that voice will be silenced."

—Vincent Van Gogh, Postimpressionist artist

What do you look for in a leader? That's the question that IBM asked over 1,500 CEOs in a survey called "Capitalizing on Complexity." From Dubai to Dubuque, and everywhere in between, CEOs weighed in on the most important aspect of leadership. These leaders from the C-suite talked about what they really want. What they uncovered may surprise you.

According to IBM's findings, the most-desired quality or characteristic was not technical competence. It wasn't loyalty, or communication skills, or financial acumen. The top characteristic wasn't charisma. Or empathy.

The number-one most important characteristic for business leaders?

Creativity

That characteristic is quite surprising, when you consider the traditional definitions of creativity. "Creative" skills are not commonplace in shipping, accounts payable, or operations. Or are they? For financial professionals, project managers, executives, and other task- or numbers-oriented individuals, the call for creativity seems quite contrary to the training and experiences that form the very foundation of the business world.

Creativity, in the context of business, means *the power of creation*. Creativity is the way we harness our imaginations to disrupt the status quo and to find new solutions to the same old problems. The global leaders in the IBM survey seek creative solutions to experiment and innovate. The leaders in the survey identify creativity as the antidote for the status quo, and central to the necessary disruption that is required for our collective marketplace to get unstuck.

Creativity can exist anywhere a process is created or improved. That means in shipping, accounts payable, or operations. Creativity means many things, but at its core, the process of creation begins with an idea. What comes to mind when you think of creativity?

I asked my friend, Adam Rifkin, about the intersection of leadership and creativity. Rifkin is an independent film producer, writer, and director, known for the cult classics *The Dark Backward, Detroit Rock City* and *The Chase* starring Charlie Sheen. As a kid growing up in the Chicago suburbs, Rifkin was practicing for his career in Hollywood by making movies with his junior high pals. If you could ride your bike to Adam's house, you could be in a movie.

Rifkin commandeered his father's video camera and began producing middle-school masterpieces like *Murder Can Kill You, Paperboy Crimes*, and *The Burglar from Out of the Dishwasher*. Adam explained, "I didn't realize it at the time, but out of necessity I was actually teaching myself the basic principles of leadership." Even at an early age, he had a knack for getting his fellow middle-schoolers excited about the next opus.

"My enthusiasm must've been infectious because each project began the same way: I'd tell my core company that I had a cool idea for a new movie. This was inevitably met with a chorus of 'no thanks,' 'not this time,' and 'I've got soccer practice.' Yet somehow, after a few

more minutes of colorful discussion, where I'd wax poetic about the
glories of the new idea and the fun that was going to be had bringing
it to life, everyone signed on again."

What was the secret to getting people to say yes?

"Here's what I knew, beyond a shadow of a doubt: If it were to
cease to be fun, my team would disperse. As a leader, even when I didn't
really know what that word meant, I had to develop a unique set of
skills that enabled me to be able to speak to each cast and crew member
individually. I had to get the most out of them creatively, also keep them
engaged." And that's where leadership and creativity came together.

From backyard movies to the back lot in Hollywood, cut to
Rifkin's latest project, *The Last Movie Star,* featuring his childhood
idol, Burt Reynolds. "Burt Reynolds was my hero. Not only was he
the biggest movie star in the world when I was a kid, he was funny
and self-deprecating and approachable. He made being famous seem
fun, and I dreamt that someday we'd not only be friends, but that we
would work together," Adam shared. A film buff from a very young
age, *Smokey and the Bandit* made a lasting impression on Adam.

"I wanted to create a role that would remind movie fans just
how great an actor Burt Reynolds is. Selfishly, I also wanted to make
good on my secret dream of getting to work with The Bandit. I didn't
know Burt, but I felt it was worth rolling the dice, so after writing the
script I submitted it to his manager. I shared my passion for all things
Burt and asked him to please send Burt the script. I also told him to
let Burt know that if he wasn't interested in playing the role I wasn't
going to make the film. I wrote it solely for Burt. My impassioned
pitch was apparently enough for Burt's manager to agree to send over
the screenplay that day.

"Much to my shock and delight, the next afternoon I got a
call from none other than Burt Reynolds. I recognized his voice
immediately and was star-struck. Now, I've met many famous people
along my Hollywood travails, but Burt Reynolds looms larger than

any of the rest for me. Suddenly I was transported to that fateful day in 1977 when I was watching *Smokey and the Bandit* for the first time and dreaming of Burt and me becoming pals. And now, here I was, talking to the man himself.

"Little did I know in that instant, things were about to get a whole lot more Burtastic. Burt accepted the role and attached himself to play Vic Edwards. My 12-year-old self was doing back flips. It seemed my dream was destined to come true. The only thing left to do was everything."

An initial success created a new vision—namely, how to fund this project.

"When I approached Burt I didn't have any of the money secured to make the film. I naïvely believed that with Burt attached to this particular script, in this particular role, at this particular time in his life, finding the cash would be easy. I was wrong. It ultimately took more than seven years to finally find the money," Adam explained.

A creative journey indeed. How can you maintain your vision, even when it seems that you're not getting closer to your goal?

"It had almost been green lit multiple times along the way, but each incarnation fell through. Every time the financing dropped out I had to call Burt and give him the bad news. I always expected him to use each disappointment as his opportunity to graciously bow out, but instead, each time the financing disappeared, Burt seemed more determined than ever to stick with the project and see it through to fruition. His enthusiasm inspired me, just as I believe my enthusiasm inspired him."

Enthusiasm?

"Each cast and crewmember is required to focus on a particular task that services the whole. As the director, it's my job to not only keep a focus on the individual components needed, but more importantly, keep an eye on the macro task of how all these countless pieces will fit together. From carpenters to fine artists to performers to financiers, a movie brings together a very disparate group of individuals who might otherwise never have a reason to interact. The director needs to not only understand how to best communicate with each individual, but also inspire this eclectic team to work well together to essentially create this temporary moviemaking bio-machine."

From childhood dream to reality: a lifetime of leadership lessons on contagious enthusiasm and a seven-year journey to bring this project to the screen. From a place of understanding, Rifkin made it all fit together.

"Leading by example and being passionate and enthusiastic about a project is fundamental to getting the very best out of your crew," according to Adam.

Fun is what makes it functional, when it comes to making movies. What about in your industry? Rifkin points to loving his work, time and time again. From that place he found new results for himself, his crew, and his actors. "The director needs to be well versed in how to talk to all manner of cast and crew member to get the very best out of him or her."

Do you see the creative spirit inside of yourself? Whether you are making movies or making gadgets, your creative spirit is what makes a difference. In fact, that creative spirit is the foundation of leadership.

A large portion of my work allows me to work with engineers across a variety of disciplines. From materials management to complex electrical engineering, my engineering clients are some of the most creative people I have ever worked with, and I'll tell you why.

Because the engineer sees things that others don't. I see two land masses, separated by a body of water, but the structural engineer sees the bridge that could connect the two.

Creativity—the process of creation—is alive and well in every client I see.

But where, exactly, does creativity come from? Let me break it down for you: *I don't know.*

I'd like to tell you that all great ideas come from working out, or taking a bike ride, or watching a movie starring Burt Reynolds. Sometimes ideas show up in those places. But sometimes they don't. Creativity isn't a place or a scenario.

Creativity comes from one place, and it's a bit of a mystery to me, but as near as I can tell, all creative endeavors start here: *inside of you.*

Every book ever written, including this one, started at the same place: a blank page. Where do the words come from? When I really stop to think about it (which, by the way, causes the words to stop so that I can think about it), the answer is: I honestly don't know.

Sometimes I look back at a chapter and I think: "Wow. Did I do that?"

Have you ever had that feeling?

That's the spark of creation that's inside each of us—that touchpoint of the divine in you and me that allows us to create new relationships, new business ideas, new investment opportunities. . . .

What if I told you there is just a little spark of God inside of you? I'm not trying to shift gears to a religious book. I'm just saying what I see. There is a power all around us. This unseen power makes flowers bloom and your food digest and your thoughts flow. It is, to me, the power of God. But you can call it spirit, or Universal Mind, or whatever you'd like.

Let's not get lost on labels. Creation is happening all around us. And inside us. Could it be that you are God? Look closely and you will see that you are the co-creator of your universe.

We create relationships, partnerships, business ideas, legal structures, political parties, little leagues, international organizations, and more. Creativity is a power we all possess. Whatever the power is that makes seeds turn into trees, and brings people and opportunity into my life ... well, there seems to be an order and a power behind this whole thing called life.

Inside your humanity you will see divinity, if you look closely enough. There's no denying that creativity—the power of creation—is in you, right now. That spark of God could be all it takes to remember what you're made of.

It's a weird thing, touching just a part of God. It's like touching a part of the Internet: you get instant access to the whole thing.

In fact, is there anything that we can't create? The limits of possibility continue to expand with advancements in AI, robotics, science, and medicine. Go to a museum, see a Broadway show, or attend a concert by your favorite performer: Where did all that stuff come from?

Behind everything you see, hear, and experience is the driving force that makes us who we are: creativity—the ability to create something from nothing.

Look around, and you will see it every day.

You could say that leadership is the ultimate creative expression in business, because the leader is the one who creates new possibilities. New impact. New ways of looking at the same old problems. The leader shares that creative vision in a way that makes others say, "Tell me more."

So, what is it that you would like to create today?

Stanislavski said, "What if?" opens the door to imagination. He called this question the "magic if." In that context, your imagination might just be the most powerful tool in your possession. You can harness the power behind "what if" right now.

But don't keep it to yourself. Ask your team. Ask your partners. Ask others to take a look in the direction of what if.

New solutions can only come from within the realm of new ideas. As the economy continues to expand, the leaders of tomorrow are the ones who are open to new concepts, new perspectives, and new solutions. Seeing things as they are can be an important skill (awareness, acknowledgment), but seeing things as they could be—and then making them that way—well, that takes some creativity.

You have to be able to ask yourself, "What if . . . ?" if you want to uncover what's next for you. Are you ready to take that journey?

It begins with a simple question:

What if things were exactly right for you, in your career and in your life? How would they have to change?

Take whatever amount of time feels right to you and write out your answer.

Now take a look at what would change if things were exactly right for your clients. Take a look in the direction of success. Ask yourself, "What if . . . ?"

Takeaways

- Creativity is part of the human condition; we all have the ability to create.
- Harnessing the power of creativity means asking your clients to be who they are—and reminding them from time to time of the possibilities.
- Creating something new isn't just a job for artists, chefs, or graphic designers; creativity is who you are.
- Divinity is inside our humanity, if we are willing to see it.

9 Information and Impact

"In ancient times, having power meant having access to data. Today, having power means knowing what to ignore."

—Yuval Noah Harari, Israeli historian and author of *Homo Deus*

The facts always speak for themselves.

Have you ever found yourself using this phrase? Or perhaps you have some modified version of it. Perhaps your version goes something like this:

- The drawings speak for themselves.
- The numbers speak for themselves.
- The blueprints speak for themselves.

Let me give you a fact, and we can see whether this is true. The fact is a number. The number is 20 percent.

Consider this statement:

A 20 percent chance of rain in Seattle today.

Would you say that is high or low?

It rains a lot in Seattle, so I would say that a 20 percent chance is low.

Now consider this statement:

A 20 percent chance of a fatal heart attack.

High or low? I'd say a 20 percent chance of a fatal heart attack is pretty high! But the number—the fact—did not change! What did?

You may say "the circumstances" or "the implications." Indeed, there's a difference between getting wet and dropping dead. I get that. But the thing that shows up for me is *context*. As leaders, we focus so much on our content. Our data. Our facts and our figures. But without the right context, the numbers are meaningless.

It's like the old George Carlin joke: "Here are the sports scores! 7, 15, 23, 9...."

Or another classic, "Here's a partial score from the Notre Dame game: 6."

Without context, the numbers mean nothing.

Leadership Factor 6

Context conquers content.

If you don't have the right context for the conversation, your data points will fall on deaf ears. It doesn't matter what you have on slide 47. Your client will never go there without a context for the journey. Consider:

- The leader never dumps data.
- The leader knows the difference between data and insight.
- *Leadership Language* models what matters for your team. You lead by example for those who are responsible for delivering data.

In my work with an international consumer finance company, I had the opportunity to speak to the organization's senior leadership. One of their key challenges? Credibility.

At least that was what showed up for them. But I saw something different. At this company, the senior leaders had to regularly present information to regulators. These government-appointed authorities were continually asking for information on the company's policies and procedures. One executive in particular felt that every response from the company was met with mistrust from his audience. In other words, his credibility was always in question.

When you are in front of the regulators, I wondered, what information do you provide? "All of it" was his response.

As I came to understand, his team would offer reams of evidence, dozens of documents, and a plethora of PowerPoint slides, all designed to answer every possible question. The response was given in the spirit of service, but it was taken as a smokescreen.

The regulators did not see the response as being thorough and complete. The regulators saw the barrage of data as an attempt to hide something, like the lawyers who provide truckloads of evidence and information in an attempt to bury opposing counsel in a mountain of paperwork.

An overcomplicated response is seen as an attempt to confuse the issue—and that complexity vexed the regulators. It's as if someone asked, "Who is William Shakespeare?" and you hand them the 1,945-page hardback copy of his complete works.

"You figure it out" is the unintended impact of the "everything matters" approach. Because if everything matters, then nothing does.

What can you do, as a leader, to find and deliver the information that *others need to know*? Listen to the words of Harari: *Leaders know what to ignore.* Taking information out doesn't diminish your message: It strengthens it!

Every conversation is selective. You select what matters most. People who don't think it through are those who ramble, overshare, and provide nothing more than a data dump.

You have to stop dumping on people. And you have to inspire others to do the same. How do you make sure that your team provides that same level of respect and insight when they communicate with you?

There's too much information, and selectively parsing to find what really matters is everyone's job right now. It's easy to rely solely on the facts to convey your message. In my experience, real leaders use data and detail to involve people in the story. Leaders focus on engagement and make sure that the clients co-create the story with them. So how do you do that?

Engaging Your Audience by Making the Data Personal

Consider a hot summer day. There are two ways of telling the story.

The first is: "*It's 97 degrees outside.*"

Factual. Actual.

But not very compelling. Weather reports rarely are.

I don't feel like I'm part of the story.

In fact, your 97-degree story is exactly what Siri just told me.

Do you want to inform? Or do you want to persuade and compel others to share in your vision?

Leadership is not about reading the news. That's why Siri isn't in charge of a $3 billion multinational corporation. At least not yet. There's still not an app for that.

Here's the second way of telling the story. It goes something like this: "You know that feeling when you walk outside of your nice air-conditioned office, and the minute the door closes behind you, you can feel your shirt start to stick to you. Ugh. Then, you see that your car is parked two blocks away. The sun is beating down on your face and you're wondering why you left your sunglasses in your car this morning...."

It's still 97 degrees outside. But in the second scenario, there are more than facts to consider.

- You are a part of the story: this story makes the second person first. The second person is you: "*You* know that feeling...."
- The story begins with what you already know. The context of the sticky shirt is one that anyone (except Tarzan) can relate to.
- The second story uses sensory words: *feeling* your shirt, *seeing* that your car is parked far away. The language is more immersive. More descriptive. The words make you think! I mean, why do you have to park two blocks away from your office? Maybe your sunglasses are lying on the dashboard. If they are, those glasses are going to be hot—so hot they might even burn your face when you put them on!

Leadership Factor 7

Leadership language gets your clients involved in the story
and gets them thinking about the outcome.

The facts never speak for themselves. They never tell the full story. Context makes your point and brings the data to life.

1. Don't embellish, and don't exaggerate, but create the context that your clients need to always *put themselves into the story*.

2. Use sensory words to really engage your clients in what's going on.

3. Feelings and emotions drive action. When combined with facts, that emotional connection is the key to involving others in your ideas.

Your job as a leader is to bring the facts to the forefront, via the right context. Know which facts matter most, and tell your story in a way that involves others.

Here's another example of a simple scenario. Can you describe it in a way that involves others in the story?

"We are having our company dinner at Flavia's, and the food critics all agree that this restaurant features the best dessert menu in the city."

- You want to list all the desserts? DON'T. That list is online anyway!
- Select the information that's important and make the context relatable.
- Connect to your client: What's your favorite dessert? Why?
- How do you involve your listener—your *client*—in the story?

The secret to creating powerful engagement is something I like to call "You Language." Effective leaders know how to speak it. Let me explain.

It's easy to tell your story from a personal viewpoint. In the example above, you might start talking about how cheesecake is your favorite dessert, and you have this cheesecake every time you go to the restaurant, and you were there with Maxine from the board one night, and ... blah, blah, blah.

Yawn. Nobody cares. Facts, facts, and focusing on yourself: DEADLY.

How is your client involved? How and why should he or she care about what you ate for dessert?

What happens when you add some phrases that incorporate "you" language? Phrases like:

- Have you ever noticed....
- You know how....
- You know that feeling when....
- Doesn't it seem like . . . (the "you" is implied in this example: Doesn't it seem [to you] like . . .).

Furthering the example, what happens when your experience turns into a possibility for your client? Let me inject these ideas into a simple story about a restaurant and keep an eye out for the various elements:

> Have you ever noticed when they bring out the dessert menu how the waiter always feels a little shy about asking whether you've saved room for dessert? Well, at Flavia's they don't bring you a menu. They bring out a cart, and for one fixed price you can try three of their award-winning desserts. They call it the Triple Play, and you just point to the ones you want—no awkward questions from the waiter! There's no pressure, only choices. My favorite is the turtle cheesecake. First time I had it was on my anniversary. All I can say is "Wow!" But you may be trying to avoid dairy or maybe you want something that's a little lighter. I get that. So here's what I'm going to do for the company dinner: I'm ordering one Triple Play for every table. Maybe you want to take a look online at the menu and find some ideas? Or just figure it out tomorrow night at the restaurant. The choice is yours. I just didn't want you to miss out on the best desserts in the city!

Look closely at this "sweet and simple" example:

- How did "you" language come into play?
- How did something familiar lead to something new?
- Did the story make you think about the outcome?

- Flavia's offers 47 different dessert choices, including 15 varieties of cheesecake made with cream from Wisconsin cows. Why didn't these details make it into the story?
- What is left for the client to discover?
- How does choice play a role in this conversation, if at all?

Language to Avoid

Negatives and constants are great ways to turn your conversation into a scolding. Even if you are trying to lead your client away from a certain behavior, take time to consider phrasing the behavior in positive terms. Why? Because that's the way our minds work. We are looking for positive, clear direction, phrased in the affirmative.

For example, what happens when an idea is phrased via the negative? Imagine this scenario, if you will:

The dog is not chasing the cat.

In order to really picture this scenario, your mind has to work twice—seeing the dog chase the cat and then stopping that chase. It's complicated!

The language of leadership is about *clarity.* Don't use negatives and absolutes (like "you never" or "you always") when you want to change behavior. Tell your clients what you want and what you need. Point them in the direction of *action,* not its opposite!

Here's a homework assignment:

1. Take an event that is represented by facts, such as an upcoming event, company report, or other circumstance that could be easily described with data points.

2. Make it your mission to use "you" language and the elements we have covered so far to tell the story in a way that involves your client in thinking about the outcome.

3. Selectively choose what is most important, and share it in a way that is relatable by focusing on a desirable (and pleasant!) result.

4. Consider what information you are going to share and what information you want your client to discover.

5. How complex is your story? If you can't execute this activity in under two minutes, you're missing the mark. The simplest message is the strongest!

Takeaways

- "You" language comes to life when you make the second person first.

- Avoid negatives and absolutes, like "you never ..." or "you don't..." when using "you" language.

- Facts are important, but involving others in the story is the key to bringing the facts to life—while avoiding a weather report.

- Frame actions in a positive light; don't ask your client to imagine the opposite of something in order to understand your meaning.

Resource

Harari, Yuval Noah. *Homo Deus: A Brief History of Tomorrow*. New York: HarperCollins, 2017.

10 The Credibility Connection

"Some things have to be believed, to be seen."

—Madeleine L'Engle, author of *A Wrinkle in Time*

"Tell people there's an invisible man in the sky who created the universe, and the vast majority will believe you. Tell them the paint is wet, and they have to touch it to be sure."

—George Carlin, comedian

In the previous chapter, we saw how some leaders struggled with credibility. Offering more information was counterproductive. Oversharing created suspicion instead of trust. Looking at the nature of credibility, I have to ask you an important question:

How smart are you?

Now when I ask you how smart you are, I don't mean to make you defensive. In fact, my intention is exactly the opposite.

When you're meeting with someone, you may be spending a lot of time discussing your credibility. Perhaps you are trying to prove how smart you are. There are a multitude of scenarios in which this might show up for you:

- Meeting with new clients for the first time
- Meeting with old clients for the thirty-sixth time

- A first date
- Encountering suspicion or mistrust, for any reason
- Facing objections from internal or external clients
- Trying to prove a point by focusing on your experience

You might find yourself talking about your background, or the background of your company, in an effort to prove that your organization offers a quality solution, that you provide excellence in client service, or that you have special expertise.

This approach was identified as "ethos" by the ancient Greeks, who outlined three modes of persuasion. Those modes—*logos, pathos,* and *ethos*—roughly translate into facts, emotions, and personal character as inputs for convincing and persuading an audience. Ethos was the aspect of the speaker's character and credibility that made the argument either more or less convincing.

Character is an important aspect of leadership, trust, and influence. Character points to credibility. But how hard do you need to work to prove and restate your expertise in order for others to follow your lead?

I would submit to you that we all have areas of expertise, whether that expertise is in commercial real estate, technology, electrical engineering, finance, or whatever the case may be. We all have areas in which we are very strong. Yet, if you are brilliant with electrical engineering, for example, that may not mean that you are very aware of any of the aspects of veterinary medicine.

My daughter is learning American Sign Language (ASL) in school. I don't know much about ASL, and that makes her an expert in my eyes.

My friend Michael was a high school band director before he got into technology. Being a band director seemed like an impossible job to me. I mean, how could you instruct a flute player, a trumpet player, and the drum section with equal skill? Did he know how to play every instrument from the oboe to the saxophone? And if he didn't, how could he be a good teacher?

He let me in on a little secret. If he was working with a student who played the French horn, for example, he would make sure he understood the basics (how to hold the instrument, finger placement, and other elements of the horn). Then he would make sure he was at least two lessons ahead of his student.

He knew music. He knew the basics of how to hold an instrument. How to make every instrument make sound. He knew rhythm and music theory. And he was always two steps ahead. That approach made him an expert, even if he wasn't a virtuoso on the French horn. He knew enough to teach it, because he saw what the students had not yet discovered.

And his students thrived. Why? Because of his expertise? No. Because of his *perspective.* What he knew were the fundamentals—and he knew how to guide his students to new results.

Let me ask you: Would you have to be a world-class Olympic champion in swimming to help someone swim better? In order to have something to offer as a swim coach, you would have to know how to swim. You would have to know the basics of the particular strokes but, ultimately, could you coach someone to better results, even if you weren't a world champion? The answer is yes. Why?

Because of your perspective.

Beyond examples of music and swimming, think specifically of your area of expertise. In this area, you are truly at your best. What is that particular skill for you? In that area of expertise, why do you need to prove that you are an expert? You've already seen that perspective is enough. There's something more important than credibility. Something in the direction of impact that is the real source of trust, engagement, and leadership results.

You may say that you need to prove your expertise because the people in front of you are suspicious—the people in front of you don't know about your credibility.

I wonder what you are trying to defend, if it already exists. It would be like me trying to convince you that I am the author of this book. Or that I have a computer. Or that I've been to college. Doesn't that feel like we are walking into a massive "So what?" discussion? A bigger question for you is this one: What would change in the way that you communicate if your expertise *was a given*?

Your clients see you as an expert. Done. Now what?

What would change for you if you knew beyond a shadow of a doubt that, no matter what doubts might exist in the room, your credibility was a constant, like the fact that the sky is blue? That gravity exists? That you don't have anything to prove?

How would your communication style change?

You see, there are two questions on people's minds when they're connecting with you in a business context. First: Can I trust this person? Which looks like a question about credibility. (Doesn't need to be proven, but it sure looks that way.)

Most people establish trust and credibility by talking about the past. Why? Because the past is known; history is fixed, and the accomplishments of the past can prove results in the future. However, I would suggest to you that what was going on with you in 2013, even if it was a really good year, doesn't really matter right now.

Investors and financial experts will quickly tell you that past performance is no indication of future results. Just because you've been successful in the past doesn't guarantee you'll repeat yourself in the future. The inverse of that equation is also true: failure in business, relationships, and elsewhere doesn't mean that you are a failure. Or that you will always fail.

I know some fantastically successful people who have filed bankruptcy; many friends are enjoying a perfect second marriage (despite what occurred the first time around).

Harvey Mackay, the author of *Swim with the Sharks*, said that failure is an attitude, not an outcome.

Do you have a story of how hope has triumphed over experience? I thought so. Me, too. Maybe there is a smarter question than "Are you credible?" Maybe there's a more significant question, and if you can answer this question in a way that's powerful and compelling—that's when the conversation really gets interesting. That's when people want to follow your lead.

Here's that second, and more important, question:

How can you help us?

What you can create through your expertise is much more interesting than trying to prove it. And spending time talking about who you are and what you've done, well, that can be kind of exhausting.

I mean, I see that you graduated medical school. Your diploma is on the wall. You have the certifications, the degrees, and the clients. Otherwise, we wouldn't be talking now, would we? There's no need for you to read your LinkedIn profile to me. I've already seen it, and I'd like to know what's next.

What really matters is what's on your client's mind, the audience that you're speaking to, whether that's your boss, your board of directors, your employees, or even a college professor. What's on their minds is where the conversation starts.

How much do you care about your clients? Enough to put their needs above your résumé, your achievements, and your title? Enough to stop trying to impress them, and start serving them? Enough to stop saying, "Look at me!" and start looking at them?

What you've done for others may be significant. But what's right here and right now is a clear and present need for your help, your attention, and your input. There's one thing your clients really want to know, even when they're asking about your background and your credentials. *How can you help us?*

The leadership conversation happens when you believe in your credibility. You don't have to prove it. Credibility, like leadership, insight, innovation, and creativity, comes from the inside.

It's not a diploma or a certification. I've met plenty of educated idiots in my lifetime, and I'm sure you have as well. Credibility isn't "out there." It doesn't come from other people. It comes from inside of you.

Do you have the courage, and the confidence, to see that you are credible? You own your expertise. Stop proving it. Start sharing it.

Don't leave the past behind, don't leave history out, but understand the focus that will serve you most to accelerate the conversation. That focus—on how you can be of service—might be the smartest thing that you can talk about.

Credibility is really about belief—what others believe about you, but also: what you believe about yourself. Projecting a belief isn't the same as providing a solution. Leadership is not a mask or a role in a play. Leadership is that most authentic thing inside of you, offered in a way that helps your client in the most powerful way.

It's easy to believe that credibility comes solely from experience. But, is that true? Is there something more important than experience?

Consider this scenario:

A young couple wants to go out for a night on the town. They've been blessed with a beautiful baby boy, now three years old, and they need to find a babysitter so that they can spend some time together.

Next door, a new neighbor just moved in about two weeks ago. She's in her late fifties and has run a day-care center in a nearby town for over 20 years. She has advanced degrees in child care and education. She is available to babysit.

Across the street is the home of 17-year-old Allison. The couple has known Allison since she was 10 years old. They've watched her grow up, right outside their kitchen window. Allison has spent lots of time with their son since he was a little baby. Allison is also available to babysit.

Who do they choose?

Of course, Allison gets the gig. Why? Why did they choose someone less experienced? Perhaps there is something more important than experience. And leaders have to understand that part of the story.

Trust is more important than experience. When it comes to the really important stuff, relationships and trust are what matter most. You've heard the phrase, "Experience is the best teacher." But I wonder, is that true?

Let's ask Mark Zuckerberg or Michael Dell or McCalley Cunningham, the freshman champion from the second chapter of the book. The world is filled with people who had difficult circumstances, limited resources, and no experience. And those folks created something spectacular.

Just like you.

Experience is a reflection of your current level of understanding—your life, till now, shaping the way you see the world. Younger leaders you respect may not have the experience that you do or the education that you do. But don't make the mistake of labeling a lack of experience as a lack of talent. And if you are one of those young leaders I just described, don't think that experience is the same as excellence.

Creativity and innovation don't discriminate. Regardless of your experience, innovation is never more than one thought away. While experience may teach us many things, one teacher is even more powerful:

Insight.

There is a wisdom inside each of us that can show up in flashes of brilliance—perhaps you've experienced it—and it's an indiscriminate and limitless resource. Experience really means what we've seen so far in our lives, until this point. Insight helps us to discover what's next.

Experience is seen in your rearview mirror. Insight shows up when you are looking through the windshield. When you are looking in the direction of service. When you are creating that thing that is your leadership vision.

If you didn't have the capacity for insight—seeing things in a new way, based on the way things are now—you could never move from your current position into the CEO role. After all, if you've never been a CEO before, you don't have the experience!

- But do you have trust? Skills? Talent?
- Do you have insight that you can share?
- Do you have a focus on the clients you serve, which shows that "I've thought this through"?
- Can you create value for those around you? Because that's what creates leadership—serving your clients, and your team, in new ways!

Experience may be a good teacher, but what happens when school is out? Leadership is in. Insight is right here, right now, and it's available to anyone who chooses to look. No experience required.

So look around you. It's time to get to work.

For your career, or for your current initiatives, looking at experience will only show you part of the picture. It's like expecting your title to inspire others. Your title is like a dot on your personal GPS; it just shows you where you are in the organization right now.

Before you fall in love with your GPS dot, take a pause. Solving real issues goes beyond titles and dots. *Where* you are is not *who* you are. Location is not the same as impact.

Titles give authority; true leadership must be earned.

"How am I doing?" is the wrong question and the wrong focus. That approach doesn't serve you as a leader. You're looking at the scoreboard instead of getting in the game. If you create trust and share your insight in a way that's meaningful to others, the title on your business card will take care of itself because it won't matter. Your title and your financial situation are by-products of the value you create for others. Do you see that? Make a difference for others and the value of that difference will show up in your paycheck, your bank account, and your business.

One more time: Keeping score is not the same as playing the game.

Focus on what's really important, not the by-products of delivering your value, and you will be looking in the right direction.

Consider the ways that you can build trust, right now:

1. **Honor your commitments.** My friend, Bill Wallace, has run Success North Dallas for 30 years. This organization is the premiere networking group in the city, providing connections to executives, entrepreneurs, community leaders, university professors, and more. Bill's tireless commitment to the community has helped build dozens of high-impact programs, supported local law enforcement, and launched hundreds of businesses. The group has had a profound impact on me and on my career. At Success North Dallas, Bill closes every meeting with a reminder: "Honor your commitments." What's the impact of that statement? Try it out in a simple experiment: Do what you say you're going to do and see how people respond. Then, do more. It's a curious paradox: The more you honor your commitments, the more trust you receive. But here's a key point: Honoring your commitments isn't about expecting something in return. "Honor" is about integrity and self-respect. Integrity is about character. Demonstrating a character of reliable service is its own reward. Focus on service, not on what you might receive in return, and,

surprisingly, that's exactly when you will receive the greatest response.

2. **Volunteer.** One of the most satisfying things I have ever done is volunteering. How about you? Do you give back to your community? Your industry? Your tribe? Leadership is about impact. Create it wherever you go. Find what matters to you and make a difference without expectation of reward. You give because that's who you are, not because you wish for something in return. Demonstrate your character by helping those that can't help themselves. You will find yourself surrounded by like-minded individuals, people with the same place in their hearts as you. And you will reinforce the impact you make in every aspect of your life.

3. **Pick up on the conversation.** Are you tired of being scolded for being too attached to your phone? Me, too! Guilty as charged! And so what? The good news is that this book doesn't offer anyone a spanking for too much tech time. But consider what Marshall McLuhan—the man who predicted the World Wide Web 30 years before it was invented—said: "The medium is the message." Is leadership delivered via text or Snapchat? (Let me know if you discover the "Leadership" filter on Instagram; I haven't seen it yet.) Choose the right tool for the right conversation—and the right impact. Ask yourself how far an electronic connection can take you. Even on match.com or Tinder, making the right choice always leads to a face-to-face conversation. Think about the people you wish to influence. What's the impact of that face-to-face connection? Perhaps for you, and your particular industry, face time is still just an app, but keep looking for opportunities to connect on a human to human level. Consider that there may be more to discover in the areas of trust, connection, and impact when you are in the same room with the people who matter most.

Try this experiment in credibility:

- Make two columns on a sheet of paper.
- On the left side, write down the things you believe.
- On the right side, write down the things that are true.

Beliefs	Truths

Beliefs are things that can be different for each person. For example:

- I believe I love my wife.
- I believe that all dogs go to heaven.
- I believe my kids are super-smart, so I hope they won't wreck my car.
- I believe the SPD is the better political party in Germany.
- I believe that Scotland should withdraw from the United Kingdom.
- I believe that Mallory has the skills to truly excel in her job.

Notice:

- Which column is reserved for religions, relationships, and politics?
- How about your self-image and how you feel about your organization?
- What about forward-looking statements or interpretations of past events?
- What about gravity and elements of the physical world, like the boiling point of water or the height of Mount McKinley?

Things that are true are different, because they are removed from opinion. You don't have to *believe* that water will boil, but at 100 degrees Celsius, it does. Truths are, by definition, shared under a universal perspective. There is no aspirational aspect of truth, nothing hopeful or discouraging in the truth itself. Truth just is. It's always possible to disagree with beliefs. But what about truths?

Truths just exist. Like the way a fulcrum works. Or the fact that water freezes at a certain temperature. Or the height of Denali is 20,310 feet above sea level. Truths have implications.

But it's hard to argue with what is. (No doubt some of you will try! And that's OK by me—that means you are working to discover what lies beyond your personal beliefs.)

Take a look and see whether these things are true, whether you agree with them or not:

- We all want a sense of family and belonging. True?
- Gravity causes all things on earth to fall to the ground. True?
- Some people, such as babies, the elderly, and those afflicted with disease, are incapable of caring for themselves. True?
- We all want safety in the workplace. True?

These truths are examples of something that I call the "high concept." The high concept is an overall theme or idea that anyone, anywhere can say "Yes" to. High concepts are things that people see as truths—truths that cause a positive response. Stating the obvious ("The sky is blue") is not a high concept, even though it is true.

Why is this distinction important? Because leadership is about persuasion and influence. Not stating the obvious. Leaders use what's known to gain access to what's new. And what is more known than the truth? If leadership is about getting to "Yes," why not start the conversation with something that all God's children can say "Yes" to?

Influence and persuasion are marked by a series of "yesses" (if that's actually the word for more than one yes). Let's look at what happens when you start the conversation with a yes.

A high concept fits into this phrase: "*Doesn't it seem like _____?*"

For example:

- Doesn't it seem like we all want a sense of family and belonging?
- Doesn't it seem like we all want a sense of safety in the workplace?
- Doesn't it seem like everyone wants to feel as though he or she is being heard, listened to, and understood?

Look in the direction of discovery, *right now.*

What can you discover that's a high concept?

Perhaps you want to ask your team to go through the exercise together. Maybe you want to talk about Maslow's Hierarchy of Needs. If so, your observations about food, shelter, and clothing could be an interesting start—but don't just state the obvious. Keep going. Identify high concepts that are true for the entire population. Got some?

Maybe you're wondering why these universal truths are so important. Consider the source of connection, and the importance of common ground to create uncommon results. These universal truths connect us all, across generations, titles, backgrounds, and personalities. When we go beyond beliefs, the conversation opens up to greater connection. Isn't that what we all want?

OK. Now take a look at your company and your industry. What are the universal truths that you find *within your marketplace?* If you wish to persuade and influence your clients, sharing your vision in a way that inspires action, consider the importance of the high concept. You wish to connect and engage your audience, and nothing is more compelling than the truth.

Leadership language is about authentic persuasion. Your story creates a "yes" around a compelling vision. Then a series of "yesses" brings your vision to life. You wish to get to yes? Why not start there? Why not begin with a high concept, something that anyone anywhere can say "Yes" to?

In a recent leadership workshop, I was outlining the idea of the high concept. "I've got one," a leader offered, enthusiastically.

"OK, let me hear it," I replied.

He stood up and said, "Do you have kids?"

Full stop. Either/or statements are not high concepts. Why give someone an opportunity to opt out of your conversation?

Universal truths are easily seen by everyone (that's why they are universal). You're not being pushy when you ask people to see what we all recognize. You're acknowledging their expertise in a simple conversation about the way the world works.

Are you with me?

High concepts point to the connections that we all share, the aspects of the human condition that go beyond personal beliefs, if/then statements, or other qualifiers.

It's hard to ignore that level of authenticity. Sincerely pointing in the direction of something we all know to be true—a high concept—is a great starting place for a new kind of conversation. And the high concept leverages what we have discussed in prior chapters:

- The high concept leverages what's known to get to what's new.
- The high concept requires authenticity and sincerity, but that's easy to find when you are talking about the way things are.
- "I've thought this through" and "you language" are implied in every high concept.
- You demonstrate your experience when you acknowledge the viewpoints of others. You leverage the power of acknowledgment

and recognize your clients' expertise. ("You know this is true" is the exact opposite of "Let me tell you what you don't know.")

- Your experience is put into action, and that's how your experience creates trust, when you begin with something that we all know is true.

- We trust and follow those who see things from a similar perspective. The friendships you treasure (your golfing buddies or shopping pals or Facebook friends or mastermind group or whatever friendships matter) are based on a *common perspective.* That common perspective is the connection that binds you to your partner, your husband, and your company. Why do we treasure relationships from college, from high school, from our home towns, or from our previous companies? Because we have a shared perspective—a comfortable and trusted viewpoint!

- The high concept is the ultimate connector, and the easiest thing in the world to trust. Why? Because it's easy to see that it's true!

- The simplest message is the strongest. It's counterintuitive, but it's true: creating a simple and straightforward *context* builds trust around your *content.* Credibility is easy when what you are saying is undeniably true.

Leadership Factor 8

The High Concept: A common perspective is the first step toward uncommon results.

Here are some examples of high concepts:

- Success is something that's defined differently for everybody.

- We all believe, on some level, that we have to take care of the people in our society who can't take care of themselves. How we go about doing that is a matter of some debate, but we all see the need to educate children, care for the elderly, provide hospitals . . . etc.

- No knot unties itself.
- Children see things very differently than we do as adults.

And from a company perspective:

- You can't have high quality, low cost, and quick production all at the same time . . . or can you?
- Outsourcing isn't always cost-effective.
- A breakdown can lead to a breakthrough, if you approach it in the right way.
- Not all clients are the same, and one-size-fits-all client service is a costly mistake.
- Good business decisions and generating revenues are not the same thing. Not every sale is a good idea.
- The client is always the client. Especially when he is wrong.

Some things to notice:

- Qualifiers are important: Saying "not all clients" is another way of saying "some clients." Qualifiers can create accessibility and can make it easier to see that something is universal. There are those who listen to defend, and they will take issue with any blanket statement. For those folks, I offer these high concepts: "Doesn't it seem like there are few statements that really apply to the entire population?" and also "Doesn't it seem like high concepts are really determined on an individual basis?"
- Clichés, such as "the client is always right," are a symptom of unoriginal thinking. Break them open and turn them upside down, if you want to discover something new. While quotes and common truths can be a starting point for connection, don't let

clichés become a hallmark of your leadership. What others have said can be useful, but when you stop the conversation at clichés, you stop the opportunity for discovery, insight, and input. As you will recall: leaders are interested in creating *something new* from what's known, not simply repeating the past and expecting "the facts to speak for themselves"! A high concept is something we all see—and that means looking past the clichés to find the insight. Look to the quotes and truths you see, and don't be afraid to turn them on their heads. Again, look in the direction of authentic truth, but see things in a new way. That's your creativity coming to life—not creating a new version of the truth but seeing "what is" and sharing it in a new way.

- Tell your client something courageous. Ask yourself (and your team): What's the most honest thing you can say, right now?

Remember, all leadership conversations are about change, in some form or fashion. Even asking a veteran employee to perform a little bit better tomorrow than he or she did today will require a change. Improvement, growth, efficiency, profit—they all come from change.

The high concept is the gateway to the change that you propose.

Your vision, if it's going to be heard and understood, needs to contain one of these four elements. Your language needs to be:

1. Unexpected

2. Counterintuitive

3. Innovative

4. Surprising

Why? Because telling me what I already know doesn't make me say, "Tell me more." That makes me say, "So what?"

What's known introduces what's new.

The surprising and unexpected is what creates that lean-in factor that Facebook COO Sheryl Sandberg talks about. The innovative conversation is the one that makes people say, "Tell me more."

For yourself and for your team: consider what is unexpected and surprising. Remember, "surprising" like "birthday presents"—not earthquakes and tsunamis. What can you discover that people have not heard before . . . but they need to?

Some examples of high concepts followed by one of the four elements expressed above, are listed here:

- **You can't have high quality, low cost, and quick production all at the same time . . . or can you?** It might surprise you to learn that we have discovered a print vendor that is running that trifecta for us right now. But I need your help to monitor our receivables in marketing, to make sure what's quoted is exactly what we've received. . . .

- **Outsourcing isn't always cost-effective.** The counterintuitive thing that I've seen is how expensive outsourcing can be when you talk about outsourcing the assembly process. I'm going to go over some facts and figures, but first I need you to look at our vendor relationships in a new way. What started as a cost-saving initiative has turned into a money leak, because of this one variable that no one expected. . . .

- **Mark Cuban said, "Sales cures all," but there's one thing more sales will cripple before it cures . . . and that's our order entry system.** Right now, Roche has asked us for 50,000 units of AB-1 serum, to be delivered in small batches to 42 different country locations. The manual tracking on this process is going to mean one of two things: We have to hire more people, or we have to invest in better technology. And what makes sense for us in the States is not the same solution in China. Let me explain. . . .

- **Not all clients are the same, and one-size-fits-all client service is a costly mistake.** I've done an analysis of our most expensive client service engagements, and three unexpected trends show up. The first is that our highest-paying clients are also our highest-maintenance clients. Second, profitability is cratering on four of our key products. And third, field service revenues have tripled in the last 90 days. Here's why we have to segment our client service, breaking out our white-glove service and turning our inside sales and maintenance into a profit center. . . .

What do you see as a possibility for your next leadership conversation? You probably see that these statements are broad and general. That's because my story is incomplete without your input. I'm not sure whether you are an investor, a real estate agent, or a dentist. So I do the best I can—and hope you can translate these concepts into your industry, your organization, and your objectives.

Personalize your leadership journey. What's the high concept that you need to share to help others connect with your vision? What's unexpected or surprising in *your* story? And what context can you establish, so that others will engage with your ideas?

As I've said many, many times: *Leadership starts with your story.*

It's time to write yours.

Takeaways

- Insights into how you can be of service to others are more important than your experience.

- Focusing on service is more important than focusing on the past. Don't leave the past behind, but don't waste time restating what is already a given.

- Whether or not you have the right to your title, influence, or impact depends on the service you can offer, right now. What happened in 2011 is history; past performance is no indication of future results.

- Your past and your experience never leave you—you can't undo what's gone on before nor repeat it exactly. But you can create innovation and insights that expand on your prior and current experience. So, too, can your clients.

- Your experience provides a process for looking at the future: What is it about that process that serves you and your clients?

- What is it that you could change in your process to create new results? Remember, transformation is never more than one thought away.

11 Assumptions and Blind Spots

"The greatest enemy to discovery is not ignorance—it is the illusion of knowledge."

—Daniel J. Boorstin, *The Washington Post*

"Argue for your limitations and you get to keep them."

—Richard Bach, author of *Jonathan Livingston Seagull*

I recently had a scary near miss: I was turning right on to a busy street in the city where I live. So I looked to my left, where a bus in the right lane was sputtering along, too slowly for traffic. My brain assessed the situation:

That slow-moving bus means the right lane is free for me to go, I thought. *Time to turn right. Right?*

Surprise! As I slowly moved into traffic, some kid on a bike rode off the sidewalk—and nearly hit the front of my car! No, wait a minute. Let me rephrase that: *I nearly hit that kid!*

I reacted quickly, then poorly, shouting my favorite curse word at the sky. I thought to myself: *"That kid came out of nowhere!"*

At the same time, I was thinking something else: *Isn't it interesting how unexpected events leave us even more surprised when we try to make sense of things that "come from nowhere"?* Because, of course, we all know that things *always* come from somewhere.

How does this relate to business? If you're like me, you plan and monitor your calendar. You watch your data. You monitor your operations, your numbers. You take comfort in the fact that you "know" what's going to happen at your 9 a.m. meeting. And then:

- Your kid gets sick.
- You have a flat tire.
- Your business partner forgets the blueprints you were going to review.
- Life happens.

We plan, but we are surprised. And we're continually reminded that life doesn't exist on anyone's Google calendar. Instead, life unfolds in the moment, in spite of how we plan. So uncertainty is really all we have, despite the calendars, dashboards, and data we may employ. Life still reminds us that the scoreboard is not the game; the map is not the territory.

Which begs the underlying question: What do you do when something unexpected shows up? Clearly, blame-storming is not the answer; nor is beating yourself up for being yourself. (How is that productive?) Instead, it's time to see what you've been missing—that you're not broken, only human.

The trouble is, we all have a blind spot. The blind spot is a scientific fact (caused by the connection of the optic nerve to your retina). But it's also a fact for leaders and entrepreneurs: You can't see everything, no matter how hard you try. But there are ways around a blind spot.*

---

*Excerpted from Entrepreneur.com: "4 Ways That, As an Entrepreneur, You Can Overcome That Troublesome 'Blind Spot'" by Chris Westfall https://www .entrepreneur.com/article/306393

The key to discovering your blind spot, and the blind spots of those around you, is to think like an investor. Let me explain. When investors hear a pitch, it's full of forward-looking statements, projections, and prognostications. No matter what, savvy investors know this one thing: those statements are always wrong.

It's not that entrepreneurs aren't diligent in their predictions. Or that they haven't done their research. Or that they don't believe that they have the skills and dedication to bring their predictions to life.

Entrepreneurs' projections are full of holes for two reasons:

1. **The future is uncertain.** No matter how hard you try to define it, describe it, and predict your outcomes, tomorrow is always a mystery. Remember the Yiddish proverb "Man plans. God laughs." The entrepreneurial investment—even if it's a series A or B round—is always *highly speculative*, full of variables, and impossible to predict with 100 percent certainty.

2. **No battle plan survives contact with the enemy.** The Prussian military strategist Helmuth von Moltke is credited with this famous saying. When investors hear a pitch, they know that the vast majority of initial business plans will change significantly, once they hit the marketplace. Business plans will pivot (shift into a new line of business or adapt to an entirely new business model) once they enter into the "battle" of the market. Why? Because market conditions are always changing! What works in the lab might not always be a perfect fit for the real world. Customer tastes are fickle. Those reasons are just the tip of the iceberg. That's why entrepreneurs have to understand how to adapt—or die. See point 1 for more information; business plans are always incomplete because market response is unpredictable.

"In theory, practice and theory are the same. In practice, they are not."

—YOGI BERRA, BASEBALL ALL-STAR

The projections in the pro forma are, therefore, best guesses. But guessing is not a strategy. That's why investors take the numbers with a grain of salt. Instead, they focus much more intently on the *assumptions* behind the numbers.

Think like an investor: Focus on the assumptions. If you want to see what you've been missing, your assumptions are the best place to start. And ask your team members to do the same.

Are you being held back by your assumptions about what's possible? For yourself, for your team, for your organization? Have you had an experience of something that seemed totally impossible . . . until the day that it wasn't? Focus on creating that change—you've done it before, and you'll do it again.

"It always seems impossible. Until it's done."
—Nelson Mandela, former president of South Africa

Human beings, as a species, are like most mammals. We are wired to crave consistency and recognize change. Stories about change, therefore, pique our interest.

Luke Skywalker's journey, from farm boy to Jedi, is filled with fascinating changes, twists, and turns. So, too, is the leader's journey (even if it doesn't carry the same intergalactic implications). Want to tell a story that gets people's attention? You don't need a light saber. You need to focus on change.

After all, if there is something that you want in your life or in your business, and it's not here yet, you have to wonder what you're doing to keep it out.

- **Not enough money?** Find the money. What's your assumption about why you can't access what you need? What's the one thing about the money that, if it changed, the whole situation would transform from there?

- **Not enough resources?** What's your assumption about your capabilities and the capabilities of your team that's holding you back?

What if your team is more capable than you realize? What if you could outsource the skills that your team currently lacks?

- **Not enough time?** Look at your calendar, with courage! What is your assumption about saying "no"? Leaders understand how to manage scarce resources. What if you knew that refusing that appointment or event would be OK for the people you care about the most? What if you could fill your time with meetings that serve you, rather than serving other people's meetings? What would change if you let go of one obligation and replaced it with one opportunity?

- **Not enough skill?** What do you believe to be true about hiring new people, outsourcing a portion of your business, or calling a friend and asking for some advice?

- **Not the right perspective?** What makes you think you can't have another one? Listen and you will find it.

When assumptions are discovered, you have to put them "under the knife." Don't be afraid to slice open your assumptions and look at their opposite.

I know—assumptions can sometimes look quite real. But really, assumptions are just thoughts.

Remember a time when you thought you could never do something? Never hire someone? Never fire someone? Have you noticed how "never" rarely lasts forever? Have you seen that the real obstacle wasn't the thing itself, but the way you were thinking about the thing that was holding you back?

Even though your assumptions may be based on what you believe to be facts, data, and trusted inputs, they are not rules, like the law of gravity. Assumptions are beliefs. And they can change. Your perspective can shift. If that weren't true, you'd still be crawling around on the floor. You'd never try sushi, or skydiving, or avocados on your cheeseburger.

Go to your favorite whiteboard, or just pull out a piece of paper, and take an inventory of your beliefs about the topic at hand. Write down your assumptions. Look at them objectively. And if you can't, hire a coach and step through these questions for the assumptions that you see.

For every assumption, thought, or belief, consider:

- *Is this true?* What circumstances could change to make your assumption less problematic?

- *What else is at stake here?* Often, there are underlying assumptions behind the assumptions! These thoughts often reside in the area of implications. What do you believe others will say or do if you remove your current assumptions? Have you seen others act without the assumptions you identify and achieve different results? What do you believe will be the result if you remove your current assumptions?

- *Go back to one.* Keep asking these questions to explore your thinking further. Ask "What else?" Ask it again. Keep asking it until wisdom shows up to point you in the right direction.

It's best to go through this exercise with a trusted advisor or coach. After all, it's difficult to read the label of the jar you're living in.

Remember, your assumptions will look real. They will look tangible. Impossible even.

You may find people in your organization who cling to their assumptions like a brand-new baby, protecting their limits with a purple passion. These caretakers nurture their assumptions and feed them. They are not willing to let those assumptions out of their sight.

We all have assumptions—it's part of our human nature. The good news is that leaders understand human nature, and they understand that they don't have to fight it.

Shakespeare had it right:

". . . for there is nothing either good or bad, but our thinking makes it so."
—*HAMLET*, ACT II SCENE II

Sydney Banks, father of the Three Principles Movement, first articulated that "Thought is not reality; yet it is through Thought that our realities are created."

We all have assumptions. Beliefs. Opinions. All those things are part of our human nature. But they don't have to be a part of your limitations.

Want to change your circumstances? Look at your assumptions. Look at your *thinking*. Look at how closely you are clinging to those ideas and making them real. When something looks like a hairy scary monster right outside the door, ask yourself a simple question:

Is that true?

Have you ever heard—or said—a version of these assumptions?

- "It's our client service team!"
- "She will never accept this offer and come on board."
- "This software system is like cement. It will never change."
- "Those guys in the warehouse are thieves and they don't care about our clients."
- "The competition is too tough!"

Then, time made your beliefs a liar, because it wasn't the client service team, she did come on board, and the software finally changed. If you accept these misunderstandings, you give in to your blind spot.

Just because a train of thought shows up doesn't mean you have to go for a ride on that train. Thought is fleeting. If you're trapped in an impossible situation remember: *Our thinking makes it so.* You are never more than one thought away from innovation. Creation. Discovery. Find a coach or trusted advisor and engage with a new perspective. Introduce some new thinking if you want to see new results.

That one thought is hiding in plain sight, right underneath your assumptions.

Takeaways

- Think like an investor when it comes to your self-leadership: Challenge your assumptions.

- Assumptions are just thoughts. And thoughts can change.

- You are never more than one thought away from innovation.

- Don't try to fix what isn't broken. You don't need to work hard at changing your mind-set.

- Instead of visualization, mantras, or affirmations, how about this idea? Action. And if you're not clear on that first step, take a look at your assumptions.

- What would happen if your assumptions changed? What action could you take, now, when you let go of your assumptions?

12 The Unbranding of a Leader

"Sell your knowledge, and purchase bewilderment."

—Rumi, Indian philosopher

Elizabeth was perplexed. The question was a simple one, and others in the workshop had answered in a straightforward manner. But her answer was filled with rambling. She was offering the details of the inner workings within her organization, odd intricacies of internal procedures that had nothing to do with the question. It was as if she were reciting details and hoping to find an answer within her lengthy monologue. Did she think that simplicity would flow from complexity?

Perhaps you know someone who just keeps talking and talking, believing that somehow an answer will reveal itself in the midst of all the words? The question wasn't about process, or technical details. The question was: *What are you going to do differently, as a result of our time together?*

Her eloquent journey was beginning to test the patience of the men and women in the room.

The leadership workshop took place outside of Seattle. Overlooking a beautiful bay—one of many that outline that city—this group of business leaders had come together to take a candid and frank look at their businesses. I was leading the workshop, one of the dozens I conduct each year through Vistage. (If you're not familiar with this international organization, you may want to visit vistage.com. With over 20,000 members, Vistage is dedicated to helping business leaders, entrepreneurs, and executives to create new results across all areas of business.)

For most of the folks in the meeting, the next action steps showed up quickly. The responses were clear, concise, and on topic. But for Elizabeth, her dialogue was dense and overwrought with history, failed plans, and rabbit holes that led to nowhere.

"I've got to stop you right there," I said. I had to cut off her response when I realized that she was actually being nonresponsive. Making words is not the same as making sense. It's important to let people finish their thoughts, but hers was a train of thought that no one wanted to ride.

"What we asked was, 'What are you going to do differently?'" I said. "Taking that question and that question alone, what *are* you going to do differently?"

The room fell silent. Emptiness filled the space where many confusing words had been just moments before.

All eyes locked on Elizabeth. She took a moment, as the question sunk in, and let out a sigh. She looked down at the conference table. She looked up at me, and the moment of truth had arrived.

"*I don't know*," she said.

Every executive in that room stopped in his or her tracks. They stopped writing notes, they stopped looking around the room. We were all arrested by the frankness—the authenticity—in her statement.

"That's the most honest thing you could possibly say," I told her. "Thank you."

As leaders, it's easy to fall into an answer trap. When questions show up, we have to have the answers. Or find the answers. Because answers are what matter, right? Being the expert is your job, isn't it?

Wait a minute. Let's take a look at that language.

Here's what I've discovered—see whether this is true for you as well. Every book ever written came from the exact same place: a blank page.

Did your sales team have a great month last month? Congratulations! Here's your reward: The month resets to zero on the first. What are you going to do now?

This book didn't come from "answers." This book came from . . . well, from where exactly? Every chapter started with a blank page. From an outline, these words take shape, but if you asked me, "What are you going to write next?" the best and most honest answer is always: *I don't know.*

Of course, what is known always shapes our perspectives. The other books I have written and published, the manuscripts I've edited, the articles in *Forbes* and *Entrepreneur*. . . . Sure, that's part of the equation. You can't disavow your knowledge or your past. But at the same time, making new discoveries means looking into the unknown.

We've seen that creativity is the job of the leader. Creating something new for yourself, and for your clients, is your greatest service. Where does that service come from? The answer, if we're really being frank and honest, is: *I don't know.*

Your leadership journey isn't a cookie-cutter copy of what someone else has done before. I know that you can learn from others, but ultimately what you discover will be your results. Not a copy. Not an imitation. If Mark Zuckerberg wakes up at 5:30 every morning and eats broccoli for breakfast, that's an interesting fact. But copying that action won't make you a billionaire.

His habits might be of interest, and they might be useful, but leadership is not about copying someone else's success. Good habits can help, don't get me wrong, but there's something else we've got to add to your leadership equation.

Your authentic leadership journey, and your impact, starts with *what you don't know.*

Because there is *power* in the unknown. The *process* is having the courage to look there, realizing this important fact:

"I don't know" is the place where discovery begins.

And as the words hit the page, or the products hit the market, or the surveys build your net promoter score, your creation comes to life.

Have you ever had a shirt with a label on it that irritated the back of your neck? I have one that has a label on the left seam, underneath the sleeve, with a spare button on it. That weird label always rubbed my ribcage, jabbing me every time I moved my arm. That label had to go. That label wasn't helping anybody.

There is a label that goes with leadership. If you see it, recognize that you don't need it. Here it is:

Knowledge is power.

That's false!

Leadership language says that *lack of knowledge* is where the journey begins. If you think a label of "being knowledgeable" is helping you, think again. (Maybe it's helping you to be more arrogant? More insufferable in meetings? Hmm. . . .)

"I don't know" isn't an admission of weakness. It's a confession of understanding. It's a high concept that we can all agree on: Every business plan ever written always started at the same place—a blank page. Or a blank napkin, as the case may be.

John Wooden, the UCLA basketball coach, said it first. Then Earl Weaver, coach of the Baltimore Orioles, borrowed it for the title of his autobiography: "It's what you learn after you know it all that counts."

Wise leaders have the courage to look into the unknown to find what's missing. The leader begins the journey in spite of not knowing. What others see as limitations, the leader accepts as characteristics. Because leaders realize that uncertainty and discomfort don't have to go together.

Uncertainty is a fact of life. How you deal with that uncertainty is part of what defines you as a leader. While information is all around us (just Google it), what we are going to create together is always in the category of "what's new."

Knowledge isn't power, unless you use your knowledge to see how things really work. That knowledge leads to wisdom.

Syd Banks, the father of the Three Principles movement, said that "Finding wisdom has nothing to do with time." Knowledge is everywhere; wisdom is what's inside of you.

Consider the insights of Murray Willcocks. Murray is a modern-day Aquaman. An extreme surfer from Cape Town, South Africa, he has lived his entire life near the ocean. Murray practically grew up on surfboards and sailboats. In 2017, his senior year at the University of Cape Town, this engineering student and a group of four friends sailed in the Cape to Rio yacht race—a transatlantic voyage of endurance, survival, and teamwork. Held every three years, the race takes anywhere from 14 to 28 days. Crews from around the globe face off against dangerous conditions, and one another, in a battle against the elements.

Aboard the *Scatterling*, a 37-foot sailboat that featured no shower, no toilets, and a tiny toy stove that looked like something my daughter received on her sixth birthday, Murray and his team set off on an impossible journey.

On their trek across the sea, Willcocks and his team of four had to sleep in a rotation. There weren't any beds on the ship—just three hammocks (Murray described them as "slings") for four men and one woman. The first week, Willcocks said he was never dry. Can you imagine the conditions?

In these extreme circumstances, where the line between life and death becomes very thin, I wondered: How did Murray find his way? I'm not talking about using a GPS. I'm talking about knowing whether to turn right or turn left in the midst of a storm. How to right the ship when nature itself is fighting against you, and the power of the sea can make your training and experience useless? How do you take the next step in the middle of a sleep-deprived pitch-dark night, where the wrong choice can mean certain disaster?

"When you're out in the middle of the Atlantic Ocean," Willcocks explained, "there's always the fear that comes into play. For me, what took over was my gut feeling: my practice and the experiences I had had before. My ability to trust myself—and my ability to trust the people around me. Because the people on this journey with me, I knew they were as scared as I was."

It seemed to me that there was more to the story.

When you're in the thick of it, there's that moment where the past, the training, the techniques, the fifteen-hour days, and all the things that are part of the journey, they all drop away because you have to keep the boat from tipping over. That's what I wanted to discover. Because Willcocks might know something that could help you and me to overcome the impossible when it shows up in our lives—even if we're not trying to survive in a sailboat, without a bathroom, 700 miles off the coast of Africa.

So Murray, when that "moment of truth" showed up—and it did more than once on this journey—what were you thinking about?

- The past?
- The training?
- The trust you had in your teammates?
- Where did you put your attention, in that exact moment?

"In that moment," Willcocks said, "I found myself directly where I was. I was in that moment. What I was thinking about was . . . nothing."

Willcocks went on to explain that he wasn't worried about what he was going to do next. The moment was enough, and he explained something that might be hard to believe: He was trying to enjoy the moment at the same time.

Think of the waves, the fear, the tumult, and the storm. In the middle of near disaster, Aquaman was smiling. Why?

Murray pointed to the natural beauty of the sea. That power was all around him. The power of nature was demonstrating its strength. Dangerous, yes, but that was his journey. He wasn't fighting the way things were, because he couldn't afford to take his attention off of the *way things are.*

Have you ever experienced a moment like that? Where the natural beauty around you forces you to stop? You stop the noise that's rattling around in your head, and you're just there? Maybe it's a beautiful snowfall in Vermont. Or a mountainside on Kauai. That calm in the middle of the storm, where you overcome the fear with a simple and profound clarity?

Some of us sail across the sea or disappear to Hawai'i, Vermont, or Morro Bay to find that reset button—that clarity that nature can provide to us. What happens when you arrive at that place, marked by profound natural beauty that can't be ignored?

Who you are becomes *when* you are.

In other words: right now. You're right here, right now.

Do you know where your experience is coming from? Is it the palm trees, the people, the storm? Or is it coming from inside of you?

You already know the answer. The power of nature is always here, right outside your window, even in the plant that's growing in a pot on your desk. Can you see it? Can you sense that leadership is inside of you, right now?

In my experience, when we recognize what's all around us, we instantly access the place of a leader's greatest strength. Greatest creativity. Greatest discovery.

You don't have to sail the seven seas to find out *when* you are. You're always right here, right now. And when your thinking settles down, you'll see it. You find the reset button. It doesn't matter whether you're on the beach or on a deadline. You'll see it.

Consider some of the extreme circumstances you have faced in your life—moments in the midst of chaos where you found clarity. Guess what? That clarity is never more than one thought away. You can access it at any time. And Murray Willcocks showed me how.*

Not only does Willcocks sail, but he also loves to surf. When Aquaman looks for a wave, not just any wave will do. He's an extreme surfer, fearlessly searching for waves that are higher than 15 feet for his next ride.

I wondered, at the top of a wave, how do you know how to take the next step—whether to turn left or turn right and, basically, not die? Could there be an ideal flow state, as suggested in *Stealing Fire*, that Willcocks accessed? How did he find it? And could it be duplicated by folks like you and me?

The force of a 25-foot wave, if you are trapped underneath it, can crush someone in an instant. According to The Surf Channel, even a 10-foot wave can weigh over 400 tons.

Surprisingly, in my interview, Willcocks pointed time and time again to intuition over technique. When asked what he was thinking at times of extreme decision making (at the eye of the storm or the center of a wave) the answer was consistent: ***nothing***.

Could it be that the "flow state" isn't found using a technique, strategy, or tip, but by abandoning that thinking entirely? Indeed,

---

*To learn more about Murray Willcocks, and see my entire interview with him, check out this link: http://bit.ly/CapeToRio

Stealing Fire points to the loss of self, and ego, among Navy SEALs inside complex military operations. The team works best when thinking slips away . . . and so do you and I.

If you are trying to remember a technique at a moment of truth, you're looking in the wrong direction, according to Willcocks' self-reported experience. You can't think your way out of a monster wave; you have to experience it.

"When you see the wave coming, you know whether you're going to go right or left," Murray explained, pointing toward his intention. "Once you decide to go for the wave, you have to fully commit. You are paddling as hard as you can."

I wonder: Have you fully committed to your wave? How about your team and your clients?

What happens if you're not fully committed to the wave?

Leadership language is a conversation about commitment—a commitment to the present moment.

Leadership Factor 9

The leader accepts things as they are on the journey. Acceptance is the first step to creating things that could be.

Acceptance may seem counterintuitive. After all, aren't leaders supposed to *challenge* the status quo? Aren't leaders the ones who won't accept second best, who won't put up with inefficiencies, and who can't accept your limitations (so you shouldn't either)?

In a word, yes. Leaders do all of those things. But this Leadership Factor points toward *how* you do these things. If you care about peak performance, look at where that performance really comes from. Before you reshape the world, you have to accept the world you are in.

The Pygmalion effect is well documented in the research of Rosenthal and Jacobsen. Simply put, the Pygmalion effect states that higher expectations lead to higher results.

To be clear, I'm not suggesting that a leader needs to lower his or her expectations. In fact, quite the opposite: Hold on to your vision. Hold your clients to a higher standard. Acceptance is simply where the journey begins.

Don't think that it's all up to you or that the forcefulness behind your expectations is the only source of real results. Sharing your vision isn't the same as forcing it down people's throats.

A drill sergeant will achieve compliance. And sometimes, that's all you need. But what if you need . . . more? What if you need to capture the hearts and minds of the clients you care about?

Willpower wanes. It's not a renewable source of energy. Feeling a little burnout sometimes? That's what I'm talking about. If you're relying solely on the force of your will, you're missing out on all the resources at your disposal. Consider the resourcefulness inside of you—and inside every member of your team:

1. The power to see things as they are, and solve real problems in the moment, is the key to the transformational change you want.

2. Every change always starts at the same place: with where you are, right now. (Same for your team and your organization.)

3. Consider this equation: vision + acceptance = direction.

4. One step at a time, your direction comes to life.

For Willcocks, at the top of the wave, the only step he could take was the first one. Here's how he described it:

"Everything goes quiet. You don't even hear the ocean. It's a crazy experience. But you don't have to be on the top of a 15-foot wave to have that experience. When you find something that you truly love, and you do what you truly love, you can be in the moment and connect to what you're really doing."

Here are some insights to help you connect with what's really going on so that you can catch the next wave:

- **Take only the first step.** I don't know about you, but I'm pretty good at planning. I see the steps in a process fairly easily, and I'm able to share those steps while helping others to stay on the journey. But every journey always starts at the same place: the first step. What Murray saw, and what we have to acknowledge, is that the first step is really the only one that matters. Planning is important, don't get me wrong. And you know that Willcocks was wearing a wetsuit, his board was in top condition, and he had scouted out the locations of the top waves before he hit the beach. Planning was definitely a part of the story. But leadership is about working the plan once you have it in place. Making things happen requires that you aren't looking in the wrong place at the wrong time. Trusting your ability to take the first step, and going forward one step at a time, will keep you in the moment. It's counterintuitive for a planner like me, but here's the fact: I'm at my best when I plan less and do more. How about you?

- **Plan to fail.** At the top of a wave, Willcocks wasn't thinking about what he was going to do in five minutes. The first step was enough, and he trusted himself that the next step would reveal itself. But when? When would the next step reveal itself? When it *becomes* the first step, of course. Leaders see the big picture; they see the wave they want to ride, but they understand that this moment is all we really have. After all: if step six is well planned out, but you don't get the first step right, what difference does it make? Focus on what matters most: the moment right in front of you.

Ask yourself these questions:

- What are we assuming about our planning process that's taking us away from the first step?
- When can we trust the plan enough to take action?

- Are you OK with the fact that the plan may be filled with miscalculation and uncertainty? Are you OK with the fact that a storm may break out when you least expect it?

- What's the "wave" we want to catch? What is it, in our dialogue and actions, that doesn't have anything to do with the wave?

- What will happen if we focus our attention and resources on the first step? Can you trust yourself, and your team, to know that you will be able to tackle that next step . . . when it becomes the first step?

- What would happen to Murray Willcocks if he were trying to load a seven-step process, or 19-step plan, at the top of the wave?

- Do you have to go to South Africa to understand that intention and staying in the moment is best way to connect with your results? I hope not!

The unbranding conversation is about removing the labels and obligations that don't serve you.

I'm not saying you should cancel your planning meeting, or that your projections for next year don't matter. Don't leave your surfboard on the shore if you want to catch a wave. But hold on loosely to steps six, eleven, and twenty-two.

The only person who can remove the labels that are holding you back is you. Those labels, those assumptions, are what will rob you of the present moment. Labels take away the power of the present—and that's really all you have when you get right down to it.

You don't have to be "branded" as a planner, or an engineer, an executive, or an inventor. In the moment, you have the resources you need. Leaders know that you *can* ride the wave.

Taking that ride requires the freedom to do so. That freedom comes when you disengage from the branding that doesn't serve you, the branding that's been created from your past, your circumstances, your own self-image.

Where was Murray Willcocks' self-image when he climbed aboard that 15-foot, 600-ton killer wave?

Answer: WHO CARES?

He wasn't wondering whether he was in a flow state or whether he had enough likes on Instagram, or whether he looked cool in his wetsuit. When he was trying to keep the ocean from cracking open his skull, he was unbranded. Unencumbered. Unrestricted.

From that place, Willcocks was able to take an incredible ride. That same ride is available to you, right now. And you don't have to put on a wetsuit to find it.

Your ability to influence others, and your immediate impact, requires you to let go of the branding. Let go of the logos, the promotion, the push for visibility. You don't need branding at the top of the wave. You need to take the ride.

Solve the real problem that's right in front of you. Trust that you can take the first step. Trust those around you. Trust that when the next step shows up, you'll take that one as well. And you'll do it with greater focus, clarity, and effectiveness when you seize the moment. Not tomorrow's moment. Not the moment that's coming next week.

This moment. Right. Here. Right. Now.

At the top of the wave, share what you see with the clients you care about. Share your vision—your moment—and ask others to engage.

No branding required.

Takeaways

- Expectations begin with acceptance.

- Innovation doesn't come from what you already know.

- Being in the moment is the place of peak performance.

- Where do your creativity and wisdom come from? What about for your team? Notice that knowledge is not the same as wisdom.

Resources

Kotler, Steven, and Wheal, Jamie. *Stealing Fire: How Silicon Valley, the Navy SEALs, and Maverick Scientists Are Revolutionizing the Way We Live and Work.* New York: HarperCollins, 2012.

Rosenthal, Robert, and Jacobsen, Lenore. *Pygmalion in the Classroom: Teacher Expectation and Pupils' Intellectual Development.* Bancyfelin, Carmarthen, Wales: Crown House, 1992.

13 Putting Power into Your Presentations

"What might this look like, if it were easy?"

—Tim Ferriss, author of *Tribe of Mentors*

According to an article by Lou Solomon in the *Harvard Business Review*, two-thirds of managers are uncomfortable talking to employees *for any reason*. That's a troubling statistic. Sharing that story with others is central to your impact. That's why we've got to take a look at your delivery, to make sure your message will matter.

Kira, the engineer, came to me with an intensely detailed slide. Every corner, nook, and cranny was filled with a detailed diagram of a multistep process. Details were central to the discussion, in Kira's mind. The extreme level of detail was, she reasoned, vital to her credibility and authority, as well as her message.

But, unfortunately, I didn't believe her.

They say the devil's in the details, and in this case those details were dragging her straight to hell.

If Kira really understood her subject, why couldn't she explain it simply?

Leadership Factor 10

The simplest message is the strongest.

Density and complexity unravel your power. Simplicity creates it.

As Einstein said, "If you can't explain a thing simply, you don't understand it well enough." Not to contradict Albert, but: let's go with the assumption that you *do* understand your topic well enough. What's keeping you from describing things simply? Maybe the ability to explain something simply is the source of a little misunderstanding.

Here are some things to keep in mind before you craft your next presentation or pitch:

What's this presentation really about? If you just replied with the title of your presentation, you're missing the point. Look instead at the *impact your presentation is designed to create.* If wild success shows up, how will you know it? What does victory look like when you have finished delivering your material? Consider the realistic and desired impact that goes beyond the title slide. Ultimately, the presentation is about what action you want the audience to take when you are finished. What do you want to create? That action goes beyond the meeting. The leadership conversation is always looking in the direction of creating something new. So what's new for you? For your clients? That's what this presentation is really about!

My client, the CEO of a major food retailer, was explaining that his company had made a $1 million investment into a charitable cause. The cause was an important part of his business charter. He kept focusing on the million dollars. But for me it didn't add up. Seems to me that it's not really about the amount; for some, $1 million is a lot of money, for others, not so much. Ultimately, who cares what the number is? What could the charity *do* with that money? That was what the investment was really about! The presentation is always about impact, and that happens in a context. Numbers are important, but what's the context for the story? What can your client do differently, because of that $1 million? That impact points back to the *Language of Leadership*.

See it first. The way to structure a powerful presentation starts with what your audience is thinking, as we saw in previous chapters. That means *visualizing* the way things are *right now*. Not the way things are *for you*; visualize the way things are for your audience. Describe the picture that *they are seeing* and you instantly build trust and rapport. The impact is an audience that registers: "She sees me. She sees us. She knows our situation."

I'm not suggesting that you open with "Everyone here needs to lose weight," but the introduction of a high concept is the best place to begin. For many of the companies I coach on their investor pitches, you will hear entrepreneurs begin the conversation with a "Picture this" statement—a comment that appeals to the visual nature of human beings. The presentation begins with a visual; ask your audience to see the way things are (a high concept) followed by the way things could be (that innovative, counterintuitive twist).

Head first? No. Head second. After you create the visual of the way things are, you want to introduce the logic, facts, and figures that back up your vision. Remember, the facts don't speak for themselves. Consider the context and its importance. That's the difference between saying, "Here's the number" and "Here's what the number means to *you* . . . and the people you care about."

Heart. The emotions drive our actions, even for the most analytical among us. Leaders capture the hearts and minds of the clients they serve. That means you can't leave the heart out of the story. What's the danger in doing nothing? What's the urgency here? What's the emotional impact of no action?

I'm not suggesting that you need to cut open a vein to make your point. But if you can't share how you feel about something, how do you expect your team to feel something for you? Conviction and authenticity are the leader's most powerful weapons. After all, the things you see—that high concept and that truth—bring your story to life. Are you able to really connect with what you're saying and feel the implications of your vision? If not, your audience never will.

Think, feel, do. For every slide you put on the screen, ask yourself these three questions:

1. What do I want your audience to *think* when they see this slide?

2. What do I want them to *feel*?

3. What do I want them to *do*?

In my work with my corporate clients, we look in the direction of impact by tweaking each of these elements. Not every slide will have every element, of course. Some slides are more informational than others. Is there a way to incorporate elements of emotion and action into the story? What about combining an emotional appeal with statistics and data that drive home the point? The best presentations bring these three elements into every part of the story, in varying degrees, to create the action and outcomes you want.

Move forward, or move it out. If you can't answer the think, feel, do questions, then you should ask: Why am I keeping this slide? If what people feel is a headache coming on because your slide is denser than a neutron star, move it out. Get rid of the density. Introduce clarity. One idea, one slide. Remember the power in taking the first step. You're not here to demonstrate your ability to plan. You're here to help inspire action. Your audience wants to know: What do you want us to think, feel, and do differently?

Countdown to clarity. How would you describe your presentation in seven words? How about six? Five? Four? Three? Two? And finally, one? There is a one-word story in every presentation. Find that one-word story. Then expand on it. Rebuild it. Reduce from seven down to one, and then build it up again. You can use this strategy to help simplify your slides as well. Consider a presentation about "The Proposed Changes to the European Distribution Channel, Warehousing, and Shipping Times" as a one-word story about "Expectations."

- Two words: Client Expectations.
- Three Words: Exceeding Client Expectations.
- Then let's jump to five: We Aren't Exceeding Client Expectations.
- And we arrive at seven: Why We Aren't Meeting European Clients' Expectations.

Does the impact change? Does the direction of the presentation shift? Could you move from reporting the news to creating action from your audience? Begin with a one-word story and see what you can build!

The meaning behind the numbers. *Conviction* is the key to your success, in any presentation. We've seen that your credibility begins inside of you, with not only what you believe, but what you know to be true. That's the high concept we talked about previously. Are you convinced? That's the first step to being convincing! Something that I've discovered about sharing your truth is that it's hard to ignore authenticity. People check their phones when you're not dialed in to your material. Set the stage for the conversation you want to have: What could you do, right now, to make this next slide more important?

The first step in telling your leadership story is the story you tell yourself. Maybe you are presenting the details of the fourth quarter inventory report. But there *is meaning* behind the numbers. There are implications. Find them. If you can't find a reason for the presentation, then send out an email. It is *never* a good idea for you to read to your audience. They can read for themselves. Insight, implications, and outcomes—that's what leaders are here to describe. Can you?

When it's time to stand and deliver, consider these strategies carefully for a new kind of impact:

Don't get cut off at the knees. When I'm coaching a client on presentation skills, I ask a simple question—usually right the middle of the presentation. Hey! Hold on a second! What's going on *with your knees?*

Here's why: Often, when we are facing off against an audience, particularly if our thinking has introduced the "fight or flight" response to delivering a presentation, our knees will lock. It's true for you and it's true for me. Your knees lock, as if to brace for impact. But locked knees will lock your thoughts. Have you seen any of the wedding videos where the groom faints at the altar? Yep. He had his knees locked. And he was probably holding his breath! Locked knees actually make it harder for you to speak, and also harder for your audience to listen! On a nonverbal level, your discomfort makes the audience uncomfortable as well.

When I was a kid, I played the position of catcher on my baseball team. When there was a close play at the plate, I was the only thing that was keeping a runner from scoring a run. My job was to tag him out, but I was nothing more than an obstacle: that runner wanted to get me out of the way!

Rounding third, here comes the runner, full speed ahead. The ball arrives in my glove a split second before the collision at home plate. The runner drops his shoulder, because he's going to do anything to get to home plate safely! Here comes the moment of truth! What do I do?

Do you think I *locked my knees?* Do you think I braced for impact? No, of course not. Simple physics dictates that someone standing still is no match for someone running at full speed. Instead, I caught the ball, held on for dear life, bent my knees, and got ready for the ride. Wham!

I was knocked back, but I had known what was coming. I wasn't trying to fight a battle I couldn't win. I had an understanding about *getting knocked back on my butt.*More importantly: I was OK with it.

And guess who won? Me. The guy flat on his back. The guy holding the ball. It wasn't pretty. But the runner was *out*!

Unlock your knees. Don't brace for impact; roll with the punches. And win. Do it with knees bent. Make sure you prepare for creating an impact for the audience, with a deeper (and unlocked!) understanding.

I'm looking where you're looking. In the middle of a group presentation, when someone else is talking, where should you put your attention? The same place you want your audience to focus—on the person who's speaking. If you are the leader of a group or a member of a group presentation, make sure that everyone knows that your focus will guide the audience. The audience is looking at everyone on stage. When you tune in to the speaker, you are sending a nonverbal clue that the audience should do the same. Focus on the person who's talking, and the audience will pay you the same courtesy when it's your turn.

It's not a presentation. A leader at a consumer finance company was having a peculiar challenge in his presentation. He was facing a really tough audience, and he couldn't figure out what to do. This executive vice president regularly presented to board members. The board had requested a presentation on his company policies, procedures, and compliance. He explained to me that members of the board would interrupt and interject during his presentation. He would be three slides deep and they would start peppering him with requests and queries.

The board was asking questions they wanted answered before he had really even presented any details. He said, "Please hold your questions until the end of the presentation." They did not. They were the board! They weren't taking orders from him, or even honoring his polite requests.

He was frustrated!

Why, he wondered, were they derailing him from his well-prepared, extremely organized and detailed presentation? We worked together to understand where this line of questioning was coming from.

Suddenly, he realized something new. "Wait a minute. It's not a presentation," he said. He took a moment to gather his thoughts. "It's just . . . a *conversation.*" BOOM! It became OK for the audience to interrupt and ask questions, because he was just talking with them. He welcomed their input. Their questions weren't interruptions; they were welcome guideposts along his journey.

He wasn't being placed in a position of weakness, but rather clarity. He was receiving insight on the topics that mattered most to his audience. Their questions didn't mean he was poorly prepared, or that the presentation wasn't organized, or that he hadn't included the details his audience required. (Do you see the thinking there?)

Actually, his thinking had been holding him back. When he saw the presentation as a conversation, he really was ready for anything, and if he wasn't, he knew it was OK to let them know that he would get back in touch with any answer he didn't have at his fingertips.

When my client was able to detach from his attachment to all of his slides and see that the conversation was what mattered, the impact of the presentation shifted completely. The adversarial nature of the presentation was gone; a simple and welcome dialogue had taken its place. The conversation is always the goal, no matter how many slides you have prepared. Because a leader looks at impact, not a preset agenda, as the true measure of success. Sometimes you discover an unexpected path, and that is actually the fastest way to an important destination.

Make sure you allow for your presentation to become a conversation. That may mean stopping and asking questions along the way:

- Does that last statement fit with your expectations for what we are going to cover?
- What else should we be looking at in order to achieve your goals?
- Let's stop right there and check my assumptions. Are we on track?
- I'd like to create a shared agenda. What additional items would you like to add?

Letting the inmates run the asylum. Asking questions of your audience can be valuable and insightful. And it can also be a very slippery slope, because what people ask for and what they really need can be two very different things. Audience feedback can derail even the most well-intentioned presentation. It takes practice and guidance to understand how to facilitate a good back-and-forth.

Asking questions serves an important purpose: clarification. But some audience members take your questions as an invitation to express themselves in a way that may seem off-topic, contradictory, or just plain *random*.

I don't know about you, but I've been in interactive presentations where some audience members just fall in love with the sound of their own voices. Their questions really weren't questions as much as they were forays into the world of story time. Ugh.

If someone's having a bad day, or doesn't want to be there, or just doesn't feel like helping you toward your objectives, or just wants to talk about Uncle Fred up in Dutchess County, that individual can run your meeting into the ditch. Have you been there before? That's why it's important for you to listen for what's necessary and to guide your audience away from what's not.

Read the room. Say what you see. Remember: What is this conversation really about? Offer options to help the team stay on topic.

You have to *lead* the dialogue by choosing your questions carefully. Often, offering either/or choices can help keep the dialogue on track. For example:

- "You might be thinking that we can't get the drug to market that quickly. Is it the distribution or the doctors that will hold us up?"

- "It looks like there's some confusion around that last bullet point. Is it the dollar amount or the timeframe that's causing concern?

- "We agreed that this meeting was going to focus on the budget for 2020, not beyond. I understand you want to look at 2021, but can we agree that this topic is the matter at hand and table your comments until we have completed our look at 2020?"

There's a delicate balance between allowing people to be heard and leading the conversation toward a desired result. I remember a time when the CEO of a company I worked for had just explained a difficult matter about upcoming product launches during a Q&A session. Grabbing the microphone, one intrepid employee said that he appreciated the explanation, but wondered how everyone else felt about it.

"I think we should vote on it," he said.

"Unfortunately, that's not going to be possible," the CEO quickly replied. "This is a benevolent dictatorship, and I'm informing you of a decision that's already been made." Not a lot of finesse in that last remark, but sometimes a leader has to let people know that not all decisions are open for debate. The CEO's decision didn't take place in a vacuum, to be fair—but not every company policy is going to be voted on by every team member. That's not efficient.

Gather diverse opinions and listen to what's being said. But lead the conversation toward the conclusion that's most of service to your clients.

Rejecting the premise. An example of an either/or question is, "In general terms, which do you prefer, something that's new, or something that's familiar?" (Do you remember that question from Chapter 4?)

Typically, when I ask that question, someone will say, "It depends." (This answer fits for many questions, especially those asked in an MBA program. But one-size-fits-all answers are not what I'm looking for.)

If you recall from Chapter 4, I went on to elaborate a little more about the premise, giving examples to put the question into context. But sometimes when you offer a context, your audience won't go there with you.

Rejecting the premise is a strategy employed by investors, journalists, negotiators, and just about anyone who doesn't buy what you are saying. In political circles, it shows up as "what-about-ism." A pundit will present a particular issue, and the response begins with, "What about [some other issue]?" For example, "The tax cuts are great, but what about our foreign policy?" "What about the veterans who aren't being treated fairly?" or some other remark designed to shift the subject.

What-about-ism is a way of rejecting the premise—the premise that your topic is valid and worthy of further dialogue.

In business, the process goes like this: You offer up a context, such as "Based on our current research, the Millennial demographic will continue to be the home of our most important consumer." And someone says your research is wrong. How you define "important" is wrong. Your findings have been wrong in the past and they are wrong again now. What about Gen X? What about Boomers? Ah yes, the rejected premise leads to what-about-ism.

Rejecting the premise is a central strategy for an argument, and it's a powerful one. Why? Because of the *fruit of the poison tree.* If you have a poison tree, everything that comes off of it is poison as well. Your argument is poison, because it is the fruit of the poison tree. So what can you do when the premise is rejected?

- **Reframe the premise.** Perhaps the rejection is simply a request for further clarification. Is there another way of looking at your underlying premise? Is there another situation or example that makes your premise true, or more likely to be true? As General MacArthur famously said, "We're not retreating. We're advancing in the other direction!" Don't make the mistake of advancing on the wrong premise; frame the conversation around clarification. Don't fall prey to the "what-about" question. Have the conversation you want to have. "True, that issue you just raised is important, but we aren't here to debate that issue—at least not right now."

- **"Yes, and. . . ."** Can you find a place of agreement and start from there? Example: "You may be right, that our Millennial market research is incomplete. Boomers do matter to us, **yes. And** that's why we also looked at what Gartner had to say about the Baby Boomers. . . ."

- **"Would it be alright with you if . . . ?"** This is one of my favorite questions in the face of difficulty. At its core, this question asks for agreement on two levels. First, to accept an alternative: Could you live with another outcome? And second, to confirm that the person is capable of coping with that alternative without further disruption.

You may be thinking, "Well, I don't require anyone's permission!" OK, boss, I'm sure that on some level that's true. But is it *useful*?

The words you choose will help your audience to *give you permission* to share your vision. They have to be open to that dialogue! Consider the places where this phrase might come in handy in the leadership conversation:

- Would it be alright with you if we table those issues until after we've addressed Sarah's concerns?

- Would it be alright with you if we talk offline about that particular subject?

- Would it be alright with you if I move through these next three slides first, because I feel certain that your question will be addressed. And if not, would it be alright with you if we bring it up again?

Got conflict? Get curious. It's easy to become trapped in your own assumptions in the face of difficult questions. Why? Because external questions always pass through your internal filter—your thinking. You might feel something that combines anger, indignation, fear, and a few other ingredients into a poisonous emotional stew. You may find yourself wondering if you are being attacked, by even the most innocent question. Is your authority in jeopardy? Did someone just accuse you of having incomplete information or not doing your job?

These thoughts can show up erroneously, and if you engage them, you will answer a question that no one's asked. You'll answer a question about your own insecurity and self-doubt. How does that serve your client?

If you find yourself feeling defensive, take note. Before you start to counterpunch or defend your honor, consider that curiosity might be the better approach. Where's that question coming from? Never mind the stream of assumptions that make you think you're under attack. What are your audience's assumptions?

Attack those assumptions with a keen and sincere curiosity. Listen to discover. What is it that you aren't seeing in this situation? What could you learn about someone else's viewpoint? It may not change yours, but you will move forward more informed, less confrontational, and more curious. That way, you never answer a question that no one's asked, and you keep your attention where it belongs. There's a misunderstanding at the source of the conflict. Do you know what it is? Get curious!

If they don't see it, it doesn't exist. It can be useful to confirm that your solution has been satisfied with a simple, "Does that answer your concern?" before you move forward. Expert speakers realize that even though they are saying words, their eyes are always working. You can see when the audience is confused, perturbed, or petrified. Acknowledge what you see, and see what you can do to help your clients toward a new viewpoint. There are always two presentations: the one you give and the one they hear. Which one is more important? Make sure you tune in to what your audience hears. I asked a client, "How did your client presentation go?"

"Oh great! I delivered every statistic and I finished on time and they all clapped at the end!"

"That's great," I said, "but how's your client doing? What did they really hear, and what are they going to do differently now that you're done?"

As a leader, you know that some conversations are going to be uncomfortable. You will need to deliver bad news. Don't duck. Make the hard calls and do it with dignity and respect.

Good or bad, your story deserves to be heard. So, whether your subject is filled with sunshine or rain (both are important, aren't they?), consider these important presentation strategies to create the impact you need:

Dispense with the pleasantries. Is it courtesy, or just a delay, to talk about how glad you are to be here? Don't waste too much time thanking all the little people: Mama and Papa Smurf, the Keebler Elves, the Lollipop Guild . . . STOP. Just get to the point. You don't need to kiss the hindquarters of every audience member for all the things they've done to allow you to be here. The sooner you move into your message, the better off everyone will be.

Every audience knows what filler sounds like. Don't they deserve more than your courtesy and appreciation? They would like to hear your content, your vision, and your service. Appreciations should be heartfelt, sincere, and *brief.* Because it is heartfelt—that means *heart*—what happens if you leave it to the end? How much is too much when it's time to get down to business?

Ask yourself what matters most: showing how polite you are or sharing your vision? If you want your audience to focus on the issues at hand, provide that focus *from the moment you step on stage.* Waste time with thank you's and how-do-you-do's, and you undermine your authority, your message, and your impact. If your gratitude feels like a stalling tactic, save it until later and everyone will thank you for it.

Don't duck. If you're about to share difficult news, come at it straight away. Delivering the difficult message sometimes starts with a brief preamble, for example: "Please sit down, Jessica. This conversation isn't going to be an easy one." Then, get to it. Meandering around bad news is like pulling off a bandage very, very slowly—it only makes things hurt worse.

They're all good questions. In my work with entrepreneurs who are delivering a pitch to investors, Q&A is where the conversation really gets interesting. After all, even the best pitch in the world is really just a gateway to Q&A. Businesses are funded based on Q&A, not on the pitch.

No investor moves forward without due diligence, and that diligence begins with well-thought-out questions. In an effort to be polite in the question-and-answer session, you'll hear entrepreneurs say, "That's a really good question."

Yikes.

That remark is another stalling tactic, delaying your results. You never hear an entrepreneur on *Shark Tank* say, "That's a really good question, Mark Cuban." You know why? *Because they are all good questions.* That's why he's Mark Cuban! Also, if somebody does say that to someone on camera, the gurus in the control room will edit that out faster than you can say "Mr. Wonderful."

You have to edit yourself, and it's easy to do when you see that they're all good questions (even when they're not, they are helping to guide your conversation). Don't waste time with empty compliments. Don't flatter the question—or the questioner—before you respond. Take a moment, even if it's a silent one, to consider the next step in the conversation—and skip the empty filler. Here's a better way to tackle the "good question":

"I thought you might ask that" can be a more powerful response. In my work with entrepreneurs, we look beyond the presentation and the pitch. Part of our work centers on the five questions they *hope they will be asked when the presentation is over.* We also look closely at the five questions *they hope they will never be asked.* Why? Because preparing for success—and potential challenges—is perhaps the most important part of the conversation.

Every successful presentation is a conversation. Explore what that dialogue looks like, including the questions that might show up! Harness your power of anticipation and take some time to think about the questions your presentation will inspire.

After your presentation reaches new levels of awesomeness, what questions do you wish for? What if your audience is tough, and they come up with questions you don't want? What does that look like?

Leaders think it through. Could you build a slide or two to address the questions you anticipate? Ask your coach, mentor, board members, or other trusted advisors what questions they might have after hearing your story.

Then, when questions come up in your actual presentation, you don't have to say, "Uhh . . . that's a really good question" or clear your throat or otherwise hem and haw while you stall to find out what you're going to say next.

Instead, you are prepared. You can say, "I thought you might ask that," or one of several variations, and reframe your answer accordingly:

- Our research indicated the same thing you are describing. Let me show you what that pro forma looks like on this next slide. . . .

- I was thinking the exact same thing when I was going over the presentation with our board.

- We were hoping you might ask that question. Stacy, do you want to share your findings from the Northeast territory report?

- I like where you are going with that, but we saw it a little differently.

- I thought you might ask that, and that's why we also introduced a second expert witness into the proceedings. Here's what Dr. Lipton has to say. . . .

It's no secret. Preparation for questions is the key to your success, on two levels.

First, it helps you to be of service to your clients when you have the answers they need. But, second, preparing for those questions can help your thinking to settle down, even in the face of unexpected questions. Uncertainty is everywhere, and no one can predict the questions with 100 percent accuracy. Yet, thinking things through can help you to navigate the unknown with greater clarity—and less over-thinking—than ever before.

Here's your homework for your next presentation:

1. **Eyes, head, heart.** Write out how you will share your high concept. Your unexpected vision. The logic behind the action you propose. And then take the big step: Connect to an emotional appeal that inspires action.

2. **Three questions, three answers.** Write out what you want people to think, feel, and do for your presentation. Not every slide will answer all three questions; in fact, it's better if a slide answers only one question at a time. The simplest message is the strongest. How strong is yours?

3. **Picture this.** They say a picture is worth 1,000 words. Can you use a picture or graph only on each one of your slides? Word pictures are OK, if you use 10 words or fewer. If you take on this

challenge, you will never read from your slides. Your audience will not be glued to your PowerPoint screen. Your audience will have to focus on you. You become the GPS when they are lost in the woods—not the PowerPoint. The slides are a tool to support you and your vision. You own the story.

4. **What's the one-word story for your presentation?** The simplest message is the strongest.

5. **Say it simply.** What is the one thing that you are going to share that you know to be true, with absolute conviction? Take a breath. Take a pause. Take your time. And take your conviction to your audience.

Resource

Solomon, Lou. "Two Thirds of Managers are Uncomfortable Communicating with Employees," *Harvard Business Review*, March 9, 2016, https://hbr.org/2016/03/two-thirds-of-managers-are-uncomfortable-communicating-with-employees

APPENDIX

THE 10 LEADERSHIP FACTORS

1. The leadership conversation always starts with what your client is thinking.

2. To get to something new, start with something known.

3. Your client's client sits in the empty chair.

4. Leaders listen with their eyes as well as their ears.

5. Leaders are deeply aligned with both sides of the conversation.

6. Context conquers content.

7. Leadership language involves your clients in the story and thinking about the outcome.

8. The High Concept: A common perspective is the first step toward uncommon results.

9. The leader accepts things as they are on the journey. Acceptance is the first step to creating things that could be.

10. The simplest message is the strongest.

ACKNOWLEDGMENTS

In many ways, this book was coached (or coaxed?) into existence. A village helped me to bring these ideas to life. I owe a debt of gratitude to so many brilliant and patient minds who have joined me to see things in a new way.

First and foremost, to my Supercoach, Michael Neill, who has shared his wisdom on so many levels. Thank you for your friendship and your insights into the Three Principles. To my Supercoach family, especially Kristi Palma, my writing coach: You always helped me to see the impact and to treat my book as a client. Bev Willcocks, Mitchell Bakst, Robin Taffin, Brad Gallup, Andrew Hogan, and all my Supercoach pals around the world: You have helped me to see and share my story in more ways than I could ever express.

The team at Wiley has been an incredible support system. Thank you, Jeanenne, for helping me to bring my vision to life. And to Vicki, my Indianapolis connection: my sincere appreciation for helping me to choose the words that mattered most! For all the collaborators on this project, your brilliance has made a huge difference for me.

I wouldn't be where I am today without the influence of Jeffrey Hayzlett, my friend and mentor. As a C-Suite Advisor, through the C-Suite Network, I see how leadership is coming to life for so many around the world.

And to every one of my clients, who helped share in the discovery process, I share this journey with you.

To the team at the McFerrin Center, Blackstone Launchpad, and StartUp Aggieland: Don Lewis, Shelly Brenckman, Dick Lester, and Blake Petty. I am truly grateful to work with each of you, and so proud to be a part of what we have created together. To the entrepreneurs at Texas A&M, as well as the other schools and incubators around the country, thank you for sharing your vision. Keep telling your story—and keep bringing new ideas to life.

I wouldn't be the man I am today without the influence of my father, Phil Westfall—a true original. You are a natural leader who has always believed in me and my story. I am eternally grateful for your love and support.

To my beautiful daughters, Ruby and Magnolia, you are my reason why. And to my incredible wife, Lisa-Gabrielle, thank you for a *Fantastick* 25 years … here's to 25 more.

My mom always said, "Each day is a day of Thanksgiving." Even when she was crippled by cancer, her health fading day by day, she smiled. She gave thanks for all that she had, and all that she had known. For the memories she gave to me, I share her legacy—and her gratitude—with you, the reader of this book.

You are the reason I share this story. It begins and ends with you.

Your message matters to me. Your willingness to invest in new discoveries is the reason why I do what I do, every day. I am so grateful for you, and for all of those around me (undoubtedly, I've forgotten a few) who have helped to shape this book.

Thanks to you, the story goes on.

ABOUT THE AUTHOR

Meet Chris Westfall

Photo credit: Walter Tabayoyong

How's your elevator pitch? Chris Westfall has created multi-million-dollar revenue streams for companies on four continents, with innovative new strategies on leadership communication. As the U.S. National Elevator Pitch Champion, he's helped clients to land on *Shark Tank, Dragon's Den,* and *Shark Tank—Australia.* A consultant to financial leaders and Fortune 100 companies, he's helped entrepreneurs to launch a broad array of businesses and successfully rebranded products and services around the globe. Working with thousands of business leaders, he's helped launch more than 50 companies, while raising over $50 million in investment capital. He's coached teams to victory in the Intel Global Capital Conference, the Harvard Executive

MBA Pitch Competition, and the Rice Business Plan Competition 2016 (the largest and most lucrative pitch competition in the world).

Chris's clients include HP, Cisco, Unilever, DISCOVER Card, Great American Insurance, The Jewish Federations of North America, American General Insurance, Transwestern, EY, and many more.

Focused on the leaders of tomorrow, Chris has worked with a number of universities across North America, including SUNY, The University of Pennsylvania, SMU, The University of Chicago, and dozens of others. An award-winning MBA instructor, he is the author of the international best seller, *The NEW Elevator Pitch.* Find out more at westfallonline.com and follow him on Instagram, Twitter, and YouTube @westfallonline.

INDEX

Page references followed by *fig* indicate an illustrated figure.